EXCITING
VEGETARIAN
COOKING

To my half a million readers..........

EXCITING VEGETARIAN COOKING

TARLA DALAL

SANJAY & CO.
BOMBAY

First Printing: 1988

Second Printing: 1989

Third Printing: 1990

By the same author
The Pleasures of Vegetarian Cooking (Hindi, Gujarati, Russian)
The Delights of Vegetarian Cooking (Hindi, Gujarati)
The Joys of Vegetarian Cooking (Hindi, Gujarati)
Indian Vegetarian Cookbook
New Indian Vegetarian Cookery (Dutch)
Low Calorie Healthy Cooking

Price: Rs. 99/-

Published by: Mr. Sanjay Dalal for Sanjay & Company,
314 Jolly Bhavan No. 1, 10 New Marine Lines, Bombay 400 020 ☎ 259718

Printed by: Thomson Press (India) Limited
Delhi-Mathura Road, Faridabad 121 007

Distributed by: Mr. Sanjay Dalal for Sanjay & Company,
314 Jolly Bhavan No. 1, 10 New Marine Lines, Bombay 400 020 ☎ 259718

Photographs by: Mr. Rajeev Asgaonkar

Art Director: Ms. Pramilla Fonseca

Rs. 99/-

CONTENTS

continued ...

continued ...

INTRODUCTION

This book is one more in the series of my books on vegetarian cookery. As in the past, the recipes are simple, quick, relatively inexpensive and easy to follow. They are written in simple language and if properly followed, will certainly reward your efforts with success. I would however strongly recommend that before trying out any recipe, you spend a few minutes in going through the introductory notes as this could help to avoid possible wastage of effort.

In this book, besides the usual chapters, I have included a new chapter on 'Cooking in a Hurry' which both teenagers and adults should find of great use. This has been written in response to many queries about coping with situations requiring preparation of food at short notice.

Cooking can and should be easy and pleasurable. I for one have always found it a pleasure to continually experiment in the field of cooking. May I invite you and your family members to share with me this exciting world of new recipes.

Tarla Dalal

INTRODUCTORY NOTES

Weights

Weights are indicated in the recipes in grams or kilograms (kg.) with the corresponding figure of ounces (oz.) or pounds (lb.) indicated in brackets.

Generally speaking, the weight in grams is given in the nearest multiple of 25 grams. In some cases however (viz. for cakes, pastries and biscuits), where more accurate weighing is necessary, grams have been rounded off to the nearest convenient multiple of 5 grams.

In the case of packaged materials, the net weights of the relevant packets are indicated in grams (in brackets) as a guide. Usually, it will not be material if a slightly different weight is used. However, in the case of condensed milk and gelatine, weight is more important and the indicated weights should be adhered to.

Measures

As a general rule, simple volumetric measures like teaspoon, tablespoon and teacup are used. The volumetric content of a teaspoon and tablespoon are 5 ml. (1/6 fl.oz.) and 15 ml. (½ fl.oz.) respectively. In case of liquids, the spoon should be filled to the brim whilst in case of solids, a heaped spoon should be used unless the recipe states level spoon.

Teacups should be measured full to the brim. It should be kept in mind that the measurements indicated in the recipes are based on the Indian teacup which is about 210 ml. (7 fl.oz.) in capacity and corresponding adjustments should be made if using cups of differing capacity.

In other cases, the volumetric measurements are given in millilitres (ml.) or litres with the corresponding figure of Imperial fluid ounces (fl.oz.) in brackets.

Temperatures for baking

The recipes give indicative temperatures in addition to the type of oven heating. However, as ovens differ from manufacturer to manufacturer, the actual instructions should be referred to for further guidance and adjustments made in the temperatures given in the recipes according to experience and results.

The following chart will prove of assistance:

Oven	°F	°C	Gas Mark
Slow	250 - 300	121 - 149	½, 1, 2
Moderate	325 - 375	163 - 190	3, 4
Hot	400 - 450	204 - 233	5, 6, 7
Very Hot	475 - 500	246 - 260	8, 9

It should be kept in mind that the oven temperature should be set at the required mark and sufficient time (usually 10-15 minutes) allowed for the oven to reach the specified temperature before putting in the items for baking. Also keep in mind that the top shelf cooks fastest and therefore generally speaking, plain cakes, sponges, etc go at the top whereas biscuits go in the centre. In the case of biscuits, it is best to use one shelf. However, if you desire to use two shelves, keep a minimum distance of 125 mm. (5") between the oven shelves and interchange the trays about half way during the baking time to ensure even heat to both.

Times
The preparation and cooking times stated in individual recipes are only meant for guidance in meal planning. The time for cutting vegetables has been included in the preparation time but times for soaking, freezing, etc have not been included.

Ingredients
The majority of the ingredients required for use in the recipes are easily available. Only a handful of recipes require ingredients which are available in season or only in a particular region.

The following information is given by way of guidance:

1. **Cheeses:** Unlike in Europe, only a limited variety of cheeses is available in India. For the purpose of this book, any processed cheese can be used except in the case for the recipes specifying use of cooking cheese (which melts readily whilst cooking).
    Paneer: Paneer (the dewatered form of Indian cottage cheese) can be made at home if desired in the following manner.
    Boil 1 litre (1¾ pints) of milk while stirring continuously. Add the juice of 1 lemon (or alternatively 1 teacup of curds and ½ teaspoon of salt) and stir gently till all the milk curdles. Leave covered for some time and strain through a muslin cloth. The moist solid left in the cloth is chhanna (which is in-between cottage cheese and soft cream cheese). Press the chhanna into a rectangular shape and squeeze out water to obtain paneer.

2. **Curds:** Yoghurt can be used as a substitute.

3. **Fats:** Ghee, the typical Indian fat, can be substituted by hydrogenated oil (Vanaspati type ghee) or in some cases by butter.
    Butter and margarine are interchangeable although in some cases e.g. cakes, butter gives better results.

4. **Oils:** Use refined groundnut or refined sesame (til) oil. If not available, you can use salad oil or any cooking oil but any such oil will naturally impart its own characteristic flavour to the preparation.

5.   **Flours:** The following flours have been specified in the recipes:

cornflour   readymade flour sold by that name
gram flour   besan or flour made from grams
maize flour   makai-ka-atta or flour made from maize
plain flour   maida
self-raising flour   flour containing baking powder
whole meal flour   gehun-ka-atta or flour made from wheat

6.   **Masalas:** It is recommended that as far as possible, dried powdered masalas should be freshly ground. Garam masala which is a powdered mixture of black pepper, cloves and other spices such as cinnamon is easily available, being sold in ready packets.

7.   **Dals:** The dals used in the recipes are:

chana dal   gram dal or split gram
chola dal   split black eyed beans
moong dal   split moong beans
masoor dal   split red lentils
toovar dal   split yellow lentils
urad dal   split black beans

Selective Glossary of Hindi and English Names

ajinomoto powder	a popular brand name for mono sodium glutamate (you can use any other make)
ajwain	a type of spice like thymol seeds
amchur powder	dried mango powder
aniseed	saunf
bay leaves	tej patta
chana	gram
chowli leaves	a type of leafy green vegetable
curry leaves	sweet neem leaves
dhokla	a Gujarati savoury side dish made by steaming a mixture of flour, lentils, vegetables, seasoning etc.
fenugreek	methi
jaggery (gur)	a sweet product made from sugarcane
kadhi	a gravy made out of gram flour, curds, vegetables, seasoning etc.
kand	a tuber available in Gujarat with a hard dark brown skin and purple inside
kasoori methi	dried fenugreek leaves
kulfi	an Indian variety of ice-creams, thick in consistency, which is made in long conical moulds.
masala	a combination of spices.
sweet potato	yam
papadi	a popular variety of string beans available in Gujarat which is dark green in colour and has large beans inside
papadi beans	the whitish green beans from papadi known as leelva
rajma	red kidney beans
sev	a vermicelli type of preparation made from gram flour
salt, black	a type of rock salt known locally as kala namak, sanchal
tamarind	imli
yeast	khamira

I. Drinks

FRUIT PUNCH

A tasty and refreshing punch.
Preparation time: a few minutes • No cooking • Makes 1 tall glass.

2 tablespoons orange juice
2 tablespoons pineapple juice
½ teaspoon lemon juice
2 tablespoons raspberry syrup
¾ bottle (200 ml. for full bottle) ginger-ale
crushed ice
a few pineapple pieces and a cherry for decoration

1. Pour all the ingredients including crushed ice into a shaker and shake well.
2. Pour into a tall glass.
3. Decorate with pineapple pieces and a cherry on a skewer and serve immediately.

TROPICAL DELIGHT

An unusual blend of juices. Cool and delicious.
Preparation time: 5 minutes • No cooking • Makes 1 tall glass.

1 small cup (80 ml.) melted vanilla *or* coconut ice-cream
1 tablespoon honey
8 tablespoons pineapple juice
4 tablespoons banana purée
crushed ice
a few pineapple pieces and a cherry for decoration

1. Mix all the ingredients including crushed ice in a blender.
2. Pour into a tall glass.
3. Decorate with pineapple pieces and a cherry on a skewer and serve immediately.

ORANGE BLOSSOM

Orange never tasted better.
Preparation time: a few minutes • No cooking • Makes 6 glasses.

6 cups fresh orange juice
3 tablespoons pomegranate
   (grenadine) syrup
6 tablespoons fresh cream
3 teaspoons lemon juice
crushed ice

1. In a glass, first put the syrup, then put the
   cream and lemon juice and finally top with
   fresh orange juice.
2. Add crushed ice and serve immediately.

ORANGE DELIGHT

Papaya and orange make a delicious combination.
Preparation time: a few minutes • No cooking • Makes 1 tall glass.

½ cup papaya pieces
1 cup orange juice
¼ bottle (200 ml. for full bottle)
   orange drink
crushed ice
1 orange slice

1. Blend the papaya, orange juice and
   orange drink in a liquidiser.
2. Pour into a glass, top with crushed ice and
   decorate with an orange slice.

★ Serve immediately.

SUMMER DELIGHT

Cool and delicious.
Preparation time: a few minutes • No cooking • Makes 1 large glass.

¾ cup pineapple juice
¼ cup mango juice
2 teaspoons lemon juice
2 tablespoons fresh cream
1 tablespoon raspberry syrup
2 cubes ice

1. Pour all the ingredients into a liquidiser.
2. Add the ice and mix.
3. Pour into a large glass and serve
   immediately.

COCO-ORANGE DRINK normalPICTURE ON PAGE 111

Use only coconuts with thin and creamy meat for this lovely drink.
Preparation time: a few minutes ● No cooking ● Makes 2 glasses.

1 fresh drinking coconut
2 tablespoons orange squash
1 teaspoon lemon juice
2 orange slices
crushed ice

1. Take out the coconut water and scoop out the meat. Blend both together in a liquidiser.
2. Pour 1 tablespoon of orange squash and ½ teaspoon of lemon juice in each glass.
3. Top with the coconut liquid and crushed ice.
4. Decorate with 1 orange slice each and serve immediately.

GREEN GODDESS PICTURE ON PAGE 111

A truly fantastic combination of lemon, grape and ginger.
Preparation tlme: a few minutes ● No cooking ● Makes 1 medium glass.

2 tablespoons juice of fresh green seedless grapes
1 teaspoon lemon juice
½ teaspoon fresh ginger juice
1 teaspoon vanilla ice-cream
½ bottle lemonade
a drop green colouring

1. Chill the lemonade.
2. Mix the grape juice, green colouring, lemon juice and ginger juice.
3. Add the vanilla ice-cream and pour the chilled lemonade on top.

★ Serve immediately.

CINDERELLA PICTURE ON PAGE 17

Looks pretty like Cinderella and tastes superb.
Preparation time: a few minutes ● No cooking ● Makes 1 tall glass.

2 to 3 teaspoons raspberry syrup
1 teaspoon lemon juice
3 tablespoons, finely chopped fruits (pineapple, pears, apples)
1 bottle lemonade *or* any lemon drink
1 lemon slice

1. Put the raspberry syrup and lemon juice in a tall serving glass.
2. Add the fruit and fill up with lemonade.
3. Top with the lemon slice.

★ Serve cold.

CITRUS COOLER PICTURE ON FACING PAGE

Frothy and gorgeous.
Preparation time: a few minutes ● No cooking ● Makes 1 tall glass.

1 tablespoon orange squash
1 teaspoon lemon juice
1 tablespoon chopped mixed fruit
(orange, sweet lime, apple, etc.)
2 teaspoons thick fresh cream *or*
2 teaspoons vanilla ice-cream
1 bottle lemonade

1. Chill the lemonade.
2. Put the fruit in a tall glass and then add the orange squash.
3. Add the lemon juice and ice-cream and top with the chilled lemonade.

★ Serve immediately.

WATERMELON AND GRAPE MINT CUP PICTURE ON FACING PAGE

A perfect starter for a party.
Preparation time: a few minutes ● No cooking ● Makes 2 glasses.

1 cup melon balls
1 cup seedless grapes
2 teaspoons orange squash
2 teaspoons chopped mint leaves
1 sprig mint for decoration

1. Mix the orange squash and 2 teaspoons of water.
2. Put the melon balls and grapes in the glass and then add the orange squash and the mint leaves.
3. Chill.
4. Just before serving, decorate with a sprig of mint.

1. CITRUS COOLER, *Above*
2. WATERMELON AND GRAPE MINT CUP, *Above*
3. CINDERELLA, *Page 15*

II. Soms

GRILLED CHEESE AND VEGETABLE SOUP PICTURE ON FACING PAGE

A spicy and filling soup for cold days.
Preparation time: 20 minutes ● Cooking time: 30 minutes ● Serves 6.

4 large tomatoes
¾ teacup shredded cabbage
¾ teacup grated carrots
3 teaspoons cornflour
1 small can (225 grams) baked beans *or* ½ teacup boiled green peas
1 chopped tomato
1 chopped onion
1 bay leaf
½ teaspoon sugar
2 tablespoons oil
salt to taste
pepper to taste

For the masala bag
2 sticks cinnamon, 2 cloves, 4 peppercorns (powdered coarsely and tied in a piece of cloth)

For grilling
4 tablespoons grated cheese

1. Cut the tomatoes into big pieces, add 5 teacups of water and put to cook. When cooked, blend in a liquidiser and strain.
2. Heat the oil and fry the onion and bay leaf for ½ minute.
3. Add the cabbage and carrots and fry again for 1 minute. Add the tomato soup.
4. Mix the cornflour in a little cold water and add to the soup.
5. Add the masala bag and salt and boil for 20 minutes.
6. Add the beans, tomato, sugar and pepper and give one boil.
7. Remove the masala bag and pour the soup into a big bowl.
8. Sprinkle the cheese and put below the grill for 5 minutes until the cheese melts.

★ Serve hot with garlic bread.

1. SPINACH SOUP, *Page 117*
2. GOLDEN BROTH, *Page 20*
3. GRILLED CHEESE AND VEGETABLE SOUP, *Above*

GOLDEN BROTH PICTURE ON PAGE 18

Golden in colour, equally rich in taste.
Preparation time: 15 minutes ● Cooking time: 20 minutes ● Serves 6 to 8.

For the stock
2 large carrots
2 onions
1 potato

For the topping
1 chopped onion
1 teacup chopped spinach
1 teacup milk
1 tablespoon butter
salt and pepper to taste
fresh cream (optional)

For the stock
1. Mix all the ingredients, add 6 teacups of water and cook in a pressure cooker.
2. When cooked, blend in a liquidiser and strain.

For the topping
1. Heat the butter and fry the onion for 1 minute.
2. Add the spinach and fry again for a little while.
3. Add the stock and boil for a few minutes.
4. Warm the milk and add to the soup. Add salt and pepper.

★ Serve hot topped with cream.

TOMATO, CABBAGE AND BEAN SOUP

Wholesome and filling, this soup will soon become your family favourite.
Preparation time: 15 minutes ● Cooking time: 25 minutes ● Serves 6 to 8.

For the stock
3 onions
3 potatoes
3 large tomatoes

For the topping
1 chopped onion
¾ teacup chopped cabbage
2 chopped tomatoes
1 small can (225 grams) baked beans
2 tablespoons oil
salt and pepper to taste

For the stock
1. Cut the vegetables into big pieces.
2. Add 6 to 7 teacups of water and cook in a pressure cooker.
3. When cooked, sieve and take out the stock.

How to proceed
1. Heat the oil and fry the onion for 1 minute.
2. Add the cabbage and fry again for 1 minute.
3. Add the stock and boil for 10 minutes.
4. Add the tomatoes and baked beans and boil again for 10 minutes.
5. Add salt and pepper. If you like, top with tulsi leaves.

★ Serve hot.

LENTIL AND VEGETABLE BROTH

Try out this unusual soup with moong dal stock.
Preparation time: 20 minutes ● Cooking time: 20 minutes ● Serves 6 to 8.

For the stock
2 tablespoons moong dal
2 onions
2 large tomatoes

For the topping
1 chopped onion
½ teacup shredded cabbage
½ teacup chopped spinach
2 tablespoons baked beans *or*
  tomato ketchup
1 chopped tomato
1 tablespoon oil
salt and pepper to taste
grated cheese to serve

For the stock
1. Cut the onions and tomatoes into big
   pieces.
2. Add the moong dal and 6 teacups of
   water and cook in a pressure cooker.
3. When cooked, blend in a liquidiser and
   strain.

How to proceed
1. Heat the oil and fry the onion for
   1 minute.
2. Add the vegetables and fry again for
   1 minute.
3. Add the stock and boil for 10 minutes.
4. Add the beans, tomato, salt and pepper
   and give one boil.

   ★ Serve hot with grated cheese.

FRENCH ONION SOUP PICTURE ON PAGE 55

The popular soup cooked in the Parisienne tradition.
Preparation time: 10 minutes ● Cooking time: 10 minutes ● Serves 6.

1 teacup onion rings
2 tablespoons butter
5 tablespoons grated cheese
  (preferably cooking cheese)
1 teaspoon prepared mustard
2 bread slices
salt to taste

1. Heat the butter and fry the onions on a
   very slow flame until brown in colour.
2. Add 6 teacups of water, 3 tablespoons of
   the grated cheese, the mustard and salt
   and boil for a few minutes.
3. Toast the bread slices, butter lightly and
   sprinkle a little cheese on top. Cut each
   toast into 3 pieces.
4. Pour the soup into individual soup bowls,
   put 1 toast piece in each bowl and
   sprinkle the balance cheese on top of the
   toast pieces.
5. Put below the grill until the cheese starts
   sizzling.

   ★ Serve hot.

CORN SOUP WITH VEGETABLES

A soup with a Chinese touch.
Preparation time: 15 minutes ● Cooking time: 30 minutes ● Serves 6.

1 can (450 grams) cream-style corn
2 level tablespoons cornflour
1 teacup finely chopped mixed vegetables (cauliflower, carrots, cabbage, onions, french beans)
½ teaspoon Ajinomoto powder
3 tablespoons butter
2 tablespoons cheese

To be ground into a paste
25 mm. (1") piece ginger
4 cloves garlic
4 green chillies

For serving
chillies in vinegar and chilli sauce
grated cheese

1. Mix the cornflour with 6 teacups of water. Add the paste, corn and Ajinomoto powder and cook in a pressure cooker until done.
2. Add the vegetables, butter and cheese and boil for a few minutes.

★ Serve hot with chillies in vinegar and chilli sauce or with grated cheese.

III. Salads

CREOLE BANANA SALAD

A rich salad with a tropical flavour.
Preparation time: 20 minutes ● No cooking ● Serves 6 to 8.

2 large ripe firm bananas
2 apples, finely chopped
100 grams (4 oz.) seedless grapes
   (optional)
1 small can (450 grams)
   pineapple tidbits
1 tablespoon lemon juice
2 teacups cooked rice (each grain
   should be separate)
2 tablespoons finely chopped
   walnuts
2 tablespoons grated fresh
   coconut
1 head lettuce
salt to taste

To be mixed into a dressing
½ teacup mayonnaise
½ teaspoon Tabasco sauce
   (optional)
2 tablespoons fresh cream

1. Slice the bananas. Chop the pineapples and keep aside the syrup.
2. Mix the fruits, add the lemon juice and a little pineapple syrup. Chill.
3. When chilled, drain.
4. Add the rice, dressing, walnuts and salt. Mix well.
5. Pile the salad on a bed of lettuce leaves and sprinkle grated coconut on top.

★ Serve cold.

BEAN AND VEGETABLE SALAD

You will be surprised how tasty this simple salad turns out.
Preparation time: 20 minutes ● Cooking time: 1 minute ● Serves 6 to 8.

1   teacup cooked haricot beans
2   teacups shredded cabbage
2   grated carrots
1   teacup sliced capsicum
2   sliced cucumbers

For the dressing
½   teacup white vinegar
2   tablespoons sugar
2   tablespoons salad oil
1   teaspoon mustard powder
2   teaspoons salt

1. Place the cabbage, carrots, capsicum and cucumber in cold water for ½ hour.
2. Boil the vinegar and sugar until the sugar dissolves. Then add the salad oil, mustard powder and salt.
3. Arrange the vegetables and beans in a serving dish. Pour the dressing on top and put to chill.

★ Serve cold.

SPICY POTATO AND CHANA SALAD

A very different and masaledar salad.
Preparation time: 10 minutes ● Cooking time: 15 minutes ● Serves 6 to 8.

500 grams (1⅛ lb.) potatoes
150 grams (6 oz.) white chick peas (Kabuli chana)
a pinch soda bi-carb
2   to 3 tablespoons fresh pomegranate seeds

For the masala
3   to 4 teaspoons lemon juice
2   teaspoons cumin powder
2   teaspoons chaat masala
2   tablespoons groundnut oil
1   tablespoon chopped coriander
salt to taste

For decoration
2   small onions, sliced
2   medium sized tomatoes, sliced
a few mint leaves

1. Boil the potatoes and cut into small pieces.
2. Soak the chick peas overnight. Next day, cook in a pressure cooker with soda bi-carb. Drain when tender.
3. Mix the lemon juice, cumin powder, chaat masala, groundnut oil, coriander and salt.
4. Add the potatoes and chick peas and mix well.
5. Sprinkle pomegranate seeds on top. Surround with tomato and onion slices. Decorate with mint leaves.

★ Serve cold.

FRUIT AND VEGETABLE SALAD PICTURE ON PAGE 27

A layered tropical salad with delicious dressing.
Preparation time: 20 minutes ● No cooking ● Serves 6 to 8.

2 teacups orange segments
2 teacups apple slices
2 sliced bananas
2 teacups pineapple pieces
3 sweet limes, separated into segments
2 beetroots, chopped *or* sliced
1 medium head lettuce
50 grams (2 oz.) powdered sugar

For the topping
4 tablespoons pomegranate seeds
1 teacup chopped roasted peanuts

To be mixed into a dressing (in a bottle)
4 tablespoons salad oil
2 tablespoons white vinegar
2 tablespoons orange squash
2 teaspoons finely roasted and chopped peanuts *or* cashewnuts
½ teaspoon pepper powder
½ teaspoon salt

1. Spread the lettuce leaves at the bottom of a large bowl.
2. Then arrange a layer of any fruit or vegetable and sprinkle a little sugar on top.
3. In this way, make layers of the orange and sweet lime segments, apple and banana slices, pineapple pieces and beetroot, each sprinkled with sugar (keeping aside some fruit and beetroot to make a colourful decoration).
4. Decorate the top layer in any attractive manner e.g. an outer layer of orange segments, an outer layer of beetroot with pineapple in the centre. Sprinkle pomegranate seeds and nuts all over.
5. Just before serving, pour the dressing on top.

★ Serve cold.

HAWAIIAN BEET AND PINEAPPLE SALAD

A satisfying salad.
Preparation time: 5 minutes ● Cooking time: 5 minutes ● Serves 6.

1 small can (450 grams) pineapple tidbits
2 large beetroots
1 tablespoon sugar
1 tablespoon cornflour
1 tablespoon butter
1 tablespoon lemon juice
¼ teaspoon salt

1. Boil the beetroots and slice. Keep aside a few for decoration.
2. Mix the sugar, cornflour, pineapple, tidbits and salt and cook until thick.
3. Add the butter, lemon juice and beetroot slices and cook for a few minutes. Cool.

★ Serve cold decorated with beetroot slices and pineapple pieces.

LEAFY SALAD WITH WARM CREAMY DRESSING

PICTURE ON FACING PAGE

A warm salad, rich in vitamins.
Preparation time: 15 minutes ● Cooking time: 1 minute ● Serves 6.

1 teacup spinach leaves
1 teacup lettuce leaves
1 teacup chawli leaves *or* other green leaves
1 small can (450 grams) pineapple tidbits
1 teacup paneer pieces
1 teacup bread croutons

For the dressing
100 grams (4 oz.) fresh cream
1 teaspoon mustard powder
2 tablespoons fresh curds
1 teaspoon sugar
½ teaspoon salt

1. Prepare the dressing by beating the cream and adding the mustard powder, curds, sugar and salt. Warm a little.
2. Chill the spinach, lettuce and chawli leaves for about ½ hour.
3. Add the pineapple and paneer pieces and croutons.

★ Pour the warm dressing on top and serve.

1. FRUIT AND VEGETABLE SALAD, *Page 25*
2. TACO SALAD, *Page 67*
3. LEAFY SALAD WITH WARM CREAMY DRESSING, *Above*

POTATO VEGETABLE

A spicy vegetable.
Preparation time: 20 minutes ● Cooking time: 30 minutes ● Serves 6.

For the potatoes
700 grams (1½ lb.) small potatoes
ghee for deep frying

For the stuffing
100 grams (4 oz.) grated paneer
1   chopped green chilli
½ teaspoon chopped ginger
salt to taste

**To be ground into a
mint-coriander paste**
¾ teacup chopped coriander
2   tablespoons mint leaves
1   teaspoon cumin seeds
2   teaspoons lemon juice
6   cloves garlic
12 mm. (½") piece ginger
1   teaspoon red chilli powder

To be ground into an onion paste
2   onions, cut into big pieces
1   tablespoon cashewnuts
¾ teacup water

Other ingredients
1   teacup fresh curds
1   tablespoon fresh cream
½ teaspoon sugar
1   teaspoon garam masala
2   tablespoons ghee

For the potatoes
1. Peel the potatoes.
2. Deep fry in ghee.
3. Scoop out the centres.

For the stuffing
Mix the ingredients for the stuffing and fill
the potatoes with this mixture.

How to proceed
1. Heat the ghee and fry the mint-coriander
   paste for 1 minute.
2. Add the onion paste and fry again for
   1 minute.
3. Add the curds and fry again until the ghee
   comes on top.
4. Add the potatoes with very little water
   and cook for a few minutes.
5. Finally, add the cream, sugar and garam
   masala.

★ Serve hot with parathas.

BAKED OONDHIYA, *Page 30*

BAKED OONDHIYA PICTURE ON PAGE 28

Gujarati oondhiya cooked in the original style and served in an earthen pot with delicious chutneys and sauces.
Preparation time: 40 minutes ● Cooking time: 60 minutes ● Serves 6 to 8.

750 grams (1⅝ lb.) papadi
500 grams (1⅛ lb.) kand (rataloo)
250 grams (9 oz.) potatoes
250 grams (9 oz.) sweet potatoes
2 to 3 brinjals
1 teaspoon ajwain
1 teaspoon chilli-ginger paste
¼ teaspoon soda bi-carb
1 to 2 tablespoons oil
a few lettuce leaves
salt to taste
green chutney, garlic chutney,
    sweet and sour sauce, sev and
    oil (optional) to serve

1. String the papadi. Do not separate into two.
2. Peel the kand and cut into big pieces.
3. Cut the potatoes and sweet potatoes without peeling.
4. Make slits on the brinjals.
5. Mix all the vegetables. Apply the ajwain, chilli-ginger paste, soda bi-carb and salt. Mix thoroughly and apply the oil all over.
6. In a small earthen pot (matka), put a few leaves of lettuce at the bottom. Fill with all the vegetables and cover with the balance lettuce leaves.
7. Cover the matka with an earthen lid and bake in a hot oven at 200°C (400°F) for 1 hour.
8. Alternatively, instead of cooking in a matka, wrap the vegetable mixture (without lettuce leaves) in aluminium foil and bake in a hot oven at 200°C (400°F) for 1 hour.
9. Serve with green and garlic chutneys and sweet and sour sauce, oil and sev.

For the green chutney
1 teacup chopped coriander
4 green chillies
1 teaspoon lemon juice
½ teacup water
½ teaspoon salt

For the green chutney
Blend all the ingredients in a liquidiser.

For the garlic chutney
10 cloves garlic
2 teaspoons chilli powder
½ teacup water
½ teaspoon salt

For the garlic chutney
Blend all the ingredients in a liquidiser.

For the sweet and sour sauce
1 teacup jaggery (gur)
½ teacup tamarind
½ teaspoon chilli powder
½ teacup water
salt to taste
chopped coriander for garnish

For the sweet and sour sauce
Blend all the ingredients except coriander in a liquidiser. If too thick, add enough water to get the right consistency. Garnish with coriander.

BAKED KAND

A traditional Gujarati dish cooked differently in a spicy and mouth-watering way.
Preparation time: 30 minutes ● Cooking time: 40 minutes ● Serves 6 to 8.

1 kg. (2¼ lb.) kand (rataloo)
500 grams (1⅛ lb.) green peas
2 tablespoons chopped coriander
1 teaspoon lemon juice
½ teaspoon sugar (optional)
1 to 2 pinches asafoetida
3 teaspoons oil
salt to taste

To be ground into green chutney
1 teacup chopped coriander
4 green chillies
3 tablespoons grated fresh
   coconut
¾ teaspoon sugar
juice of ½ lemon
salt to taste

To be ground into chilli-ginger paste
4 green chillies
12 mm. (½") piece ginger

For the coconut sauce
1 coconut, grated
1 teaspoon cumin seeds
1 teaspoon plain flour
2 teaspoons chutney
2 pinches sugar
1 tablespoon ghee
salt to taste

For the baking
½ teacup milk

1. Peel and slice the kand into about 3 mm. (⅛") thick pieces. Sprinkle salt and marinate in the green chutney for ½ hour.
2. Steam the kand until soft.
3. Boil the peas and mash.
4. Heat the oil and add the peas, coriander, chilli-ginger paste, lemon juice, sugar and asafoetida.

For the coconut sauce
1. Mix the coconut and 2 teacups of water and allow to stand for at least ½ hour. Blend in a liquidiser and pass through a sieve to get coconut milk.
2. Heat the ghee and fry the cumin seeds for ½ minute. Add the flour and chutney and fry for a further ½ minute.
3. Add the coconut milk, sugar and salt and boil for 2 minutes.

How to proceed
1. In an aluminium foil, spread half the kand slices, then spread the green peas mixture and finally the balance kand slices. Sprinkle the milk and close the foil.
2. Bake in a hot oven at 200°C (400°F) for 10 to 15 minutes.

   ★ Serve hot with coconut sauce.

CORN PANKI PICTURE ON PAGE 37

A novel snack with the aroma of fresh leaves.
Ideal as a start for a cocktail party or for a tea party.
Preparation time: 10 minutes ● Cooking time: 15 minutes ● Serves 4 to 6.

6 tender corncobs
2 tablespoons plain flour
1 tablespoon semolina (rawa)
1 tablespoon chopped coriander
2 teaspoons finely chopped green
   chillies
¼ teaspoon soda bi-carb or Eno's
   fruit salt
2 tablespoons fresh curds
2 teaspoons oil
salt to taste
melted butter and green chutney
   for serving

1. Grate the corn. To the grated corn, add the remaining ingredients and mix well.
2. Cut banana leaves into small squares.
3. Apply a little oil to the banana or corn leaves. Spread a little mixture on each leaf portion and put another greased leaf on top.
4. Cook on a tawa (griddle) until light brown spots appear on top.

★ Serve hot with melted butter and green chutney.

HANDI KHICHADI

Serve this delicious khichadi steaming hot in an earthen pot.
Preparation time: 30 minutes ● Cooking time: 30 minutes ● Serves 6.

1½ teacups rice
1½ teacups papadi beans (leelva)
1½ teacups Gujarati kadhi,
   page 120
3 sticks cinnamon
3 cloves
2 bay leaves
3 tablespoons ghee
salt to taste

To be ground into a paste
1 onion
6 green chillies
25 mm. (1") piece ginger
2 cardamoms
1 teaspoon lemon juice
3 tablespoons chopped coriander
6 cloves garlic

1. Heat the ghee and fry the cinnamon, cloves and bay leaves for a few seconds.
2. Add the paste and fry for 2 minutes.
3. Add the rice and beans and cook for 2 minutes.
4. Add 4 teacups of hot water and salt and pour the mixture into an earthen pot (or in a big bowl).
5. Cover and cook in a hot oven at 200°C (400°F) for 20 minutes.
6. When the rice is cooked, pour the kadhi over it.
7. Cover and bake again at 200°C (400°F) for 5 minutes.

★ Serve hot.

MALAI CAULIFLOWER

A wholesome dish for the cauliflower lovers.
Preparation time: 15 minutes ● Cooking time: 20 minutes ● Serves 6.

750 grams (1⅝ lb.) cauliflower
4   tablespoons oil *or* ghee
3   tablespoons powdered milk
2   pinches sugar (optional)

For the paste
1½ onions
12 mm. (½") piece ginger
3   cloves garlic
4   to 5 green chillies

For the garam masala
12 mm. (½") stick cinnamon
2   cardamoms
1   clove

1. Cut the cauliflower into florettes. Boil in a broad vessel in salted water taking care to see that the cauliflower remains firm.
2. Make a paste of the powdered milk with ¾ teacup of water.
3. Heat 2 tablespoons of oil and fry the cauliflower for 3 to 4 minutes.
4. Add the remaining 2 tablespoons of oil. Add the paste and garam masala and fry until the oil comes on top.
5. Add the milk powder paste and cook till the mixture looks like crumbled paneer.
6. Now add the boiled cauliflower and 1 teacup of water and simmer for 5 minutes until the gravy thickens.
7. Taste and if desired, add the sugar.

* Serve hot with rice or chapatis.

KADAI PANEER

Serve this dish with naan or parathas or simply as a starter.
Preparation time: 30 minutes ● Cooking time: 20 minutes ● Serves 6.

500 grams (1⅛ lb.) paneer
100 grams (4 oz.) capsicum
2   teaspoons coriander seeds
5   whole red chillies
¾ teaspoon kasoori methi
    (dry fenugreek leaves)
2   chopped green chillies
2   teaspoons chopped ginger
4   chopped tomatoes
2   tablespoons chopped coriander
3   tablespoons ghee
salt to taste

For the paste
6   cloves garlic mixed with a little water

1. Slice the paneer and capsicum into thin long strips.
2. Pound the coriander seeds and red chillies together.
3. Heat the ghee, add the garlic paste and cook on a slow flame for a few seconds.
4. Add the capsicum and pounded spices and cook on a slow flame for 30 seconds.
5. Add the green chillies and ginger and fry again for a few seconds.
6. Add the tomatoes and cook until the ghee comes on top.
7. Add the kasoori methi and salt and fry again for a few seconds.
8. Finally, add the sliced paneer and cook for a few minutes.

★ Sprinkle coriander on top and serve hot.

CHHILKEWALE PARATHE PICTURE ON PAGE 37

A very different type of paratha:
Preparation time: 20 minutes • Cooking time: 20 minutes • Makes 8 parathas.

1 teacup moong dal skin
2 teacups whole wheat flour
2 teaspoons coarsely powdered
  coriander seeds
3 finely chopped green chillies
1 chopped onion
2 teaspoons oil
1 boiled and mashed potato
salt to taste
oil *or* ghee for frying

1. Mix all the ingredients and add water to make a soft dough.
2. Roll out into thick rotis and cook on a tawa (griddle) on both sides with oil until pink spots come on top.

★ Serve hot with curds.

MIXED DAL PICTURE ON PAGE 37

A tasty combination of lentils.
Preparation time: 10 minutes • Cooking time: 40 minutes • Serves 6.

1 tablespoon moong dal
1 tablespoon masoor dal
1 tablespoon urad dal
1 tablespoon chana dal
2 tablespoons toovar dal
1 teaspoon cumin seeds
1 onion, chopped
2 teaspoons coriander powder
1 teaspoon chilli powder
½ teaspoon turmeric powder
2 tablespoons chopped coriander
3 tablespoons ghee
salt to taste

For the tempering
2 tablespoons butter
1 chopped tomato
1 teacup fresh curds
½ teaspoon garam masala

1. Wash all the dals. Soak for 1 hour and then drain.
2. Heat the ghee. Add the cumin seeds and cook until they begin to crackle.
3. Add the onion and cook until light pink.
4. Now add all the dals and cook again for 4 to 5 minutes.
5. Add 1 litre of water and cook on a slow flame until soft.
6. Then add the coriander powder, chilli powder, turmeric powder and salt. Cover and cook until two thirds of the water has evaporated.
7. Mash the dals lightly.
8. Prepare the tempering by melting the butter, adding the tomato, curds and garam masala and cooking on a slow flame for 1 to 2 minutes.
9. Add to the cooked dals and stir for 3 to 4 minutes.

★ Sprinkle coriander on top and serve hot.

PANEER IN WHITE GRAVY PICTURE ON PAGE 37

A delicately flavoured dish.
Preparation time: 20 minutes • Cooking time: 20 minutes • Serves 4 to 6.

200 grams (7 oz.) paneer
2 medium onions
1 tablespoon cashewnut pieces
3 cardamoms
2 cloves
1 stick cinnamon
1 bay leaf
3 chopped green chillies
1 red chilli
1 teaspoon coriander seeds
1 teacup fresh curds
¾ teacup finely chopped
   coriander
½ teaspoon sugar
2 tablespoons ghee
salt to taste

To be ground into a paste
6 cloves garlic
12 mm. (½") piece ginger
1 tablespoon water

1. Cut the paneer into small cubes.
2. Cut the onions into big pieces, add ¾ teacup of water and boil.
3. When cooked, blend in a mixer along with the cashewnut pieces.
4. Heat the ghee and fry the cardamoms, cloves, cinnamon and bay leaf for ½ minute.
5. Add the paste and fry for ½ minute.
6. Add the ground onions and cashewnuts and fry for a little while.
7. Add the green chillies and fry for a little while.
8. Pound the red chilli and coriander seeds and add to the gravy. Fry again for a few seconds. Take the vessel off the fire.
9. Churn the curds and add to the mixture. Add salt and cook on a slow flame until the ghee comes on top.
10. Add the coriander and cook for ½ minute.
11. Finally, add the paneer and sugar and cook for a few minutes.

★ Serve hot with parathas.

MIXED VEGETABLE PARATHAS PICTURE ON FACING PAGE

Wholesome stuffed parathas.
Preparation time: 20 minutes ● Cooking time: 20 minutes ● Makes 10 to 12 parathas.

For the stuffing
2 teacups finely chopped mixed vegetables (french beans, carrots, cauliflower, green peas)
3 to 4 finely chopped spring onions
1 small boiled potato
2 tablespoons chopped coriander
2 chopped green chillies
a pinch Ajinomoto powder
1 teaspoon chilli powder
1 tablespoon oil
salt to taste

For the dough
1 teacup plain flour
1 teacup whole wheat flour
2 teaspoons oil
½ teaspoon salt

For cooking
ghee

For the stuffing
1. Heat the oil and fry the mixed vegetables, and spring onions on a very high flame for 1 minute.
2. Add the Ajinomoto powder and cook for a further 3 to 4 minutes.
3. Add the potato, coriander, green chillies, chilli powder and salt and mix well.

For the dough
1. Mix all the ingredients and add water to make a soft dough.
2. Divide the dough into 10 to 12 portions. Roll out thinly.

How to proceed
Put 1 tablespoon of the stuffing in the centre of each dough round. Make an envelope by folding all the sides over the vegetables. Cook on a tawa (griddle) with ghee until crisp on both sides. Repeat for the remaining dough rounds and stuffing.

★ Serve hot.

1. MIXED DAL, *Page 34*
2. PANEER IN WHITE GRAVY, *Page 35*
3. CHHILKEWALE PARATHE, *Page 34*
4. MIXED VEGETABLE PARATHAS, *Above*
5. CORN PANKI, *Page 32*

EAST AND WEST RICE

Buttered rice with vegetable stew, a harmonious blend of the East and West.
Preparation time: 25 minutes ● Cooking time: 25 minutes ● Serves 6 to 8.

For the vegetable stew
2 teacups mixed boiled vegetables (french beans, carrots, green peas, potatoes)
2 chopped apples
1 chopped capsicum
1 chopped tomato
1 teaspoon chilli powder
1 teacup tomato ketchup
3 tablespoons fresh cream
3 tablespoons ghee
salt to taste

To be ground into a paste (for the stew)
1 onion
4 green chillies
25 mm. (1") piece ginger

For the buttered rice
2 teacups uncooked rice
2 tablespoons butter
salt to taste

For the vegetable stew
1. Heat the ghee and fry the paste for a few minutes.
2. Add the apples, capsicum, tomato and chilli powder and cook for 3 to 4 minutes.
3. Add the vegetables, tomato ketchup, ½ teacup of water and salt. Cook for a few minutes. Add the cream.

For the buttered rice
1. Boil the rice. Each grain of the cooked rice should be separate. Drain and cool.
2. Heat the butter in a vessel. Add the rice and salt.

★ Serve the stew hot with buttered rice.

1. QUICK MASALA SPAGHETTI, *Page 41*
2. SPINACH TARTILLINI IN CREAM SAUCE, *Page 42*
3. SPINACH DUMPLINGS IN TOMATO GRAVY, *Page 51*

PEARL PULLAV

A nourishing rice with chick peas which will prove a hit at any party.
Preparation time: 20 minutes ● Cooking time: 40 minutes ● Serves 6 to 8.

For the rice

1½ teacups uncooked Basmati rice
2 cardamoms
2 cloves
1 cinnamon
1 bay leaf
1½ teacups milk
1½ teacups water
2½ teaspoons salt

For the gravy

1 teacup white chick peas
  (Kabuli chana)
1 pinch soda bi-carb
1 teaspoons ginger paste
1 teaspoons garlic paste
1 teaspoon chilli powder
½ teaspoon turmeric powder
1 teacup fresh curds
1 teacup chopped tomatoes
2 chopped potatoes
3 chopped green chillies
3 tablespoons ghee
salt to taste

For the baking

2 tablespoons chopped coriander
1 tablespoon chopped mint
1 chopped green chilli
2 tablespoons fried onions
¼ teacup milk with a dash of
  saffron

For the rice

1. Soak the rice for 30 minutes. Drain.
2. Mix the water and milk together.
3. Add the cardamoms, cloves, cinnamon, bay leaf, salt and rice and cook until almost done.

For the gravy

1. Soak the chick peas overnight. Next day, boil with a little water and the soda bi-carb. Drain.
2. Heat the ghee, add the ginger and garlic pastes and fry for a while.
3. Add the chilli powder and the turmeric (in a little water) and fry for 1 minute.
4. Add the curds, tomatoes, potatoes and green chillies and stir for a while.
5. Add the chick peas and salt.

How to proceed

1. To the cooked rice, add the coriander, mint, green chillies and fried onions.
2. Put one layer of rice in a big bowl and spread a layer of chick pea gravy on top.
3. Make alternate layers of rice and gravy in this manner.
4. Finally sprinkle the saffron milk on top, cover and bake in a hot oven at 200°C (400°F) for 20 minutes.
5. When baked, turn upside down in a serving dish and serve hot.

V. Western Dishes

QUICK MASALA SPAGHETTI PICTURE ON PAGE 38

Cook this dish in front of the guests and serve immediately.
Preparation time: 25 minutes ● Cooking time: 15 minutes ● Serves 4 to 6.

2 teacups boiled spaghetti
1 chopped onion
1 large tomato
2 tablespoons chopped
   capsicum
1 tablespoon chopped celery
4 tablespoons tomato ketchup
½ teaspoon chilli sauce
½ teaspoon mustard powder
100 grams (4 oz.) fresh cream
1½ teacups sliced mushrooms
   (optional)
1 teaspoon lemon juice
2 tablespoons butter
salt to taste
grated cheese to serve

To be ground into a paste
4 cloves garlic
12 mm. (½") piece ginger
4 red chillies

1. Put the tomato into hot water for 10 minutes. Remove the skin and chop.
2. Heat the butter and fry the onion till pale in colour.
3. Add the celery and fry again for ½ minute. Add the paste and fry again for ½ minute.
4. Add the tomato pulp and the capsicum and fry for 3 to 4 minutes.
5. Add the spaghetti, tomato ketchup, chilli sauce, mustard powder, three-quarters of the cream and salt and cook for 1 minute.
6. Add the lemon juice and the mushrooms and cook again.

★ Serve hot with the remaining cream and the grated cheese.

SPINACH TARTILLINI IN CREAM SAUCE PICTURE ON PAGE 38

A superb Italian dish with 2 rich sauces.
Preparation time: 30 minutes ● Cooking time: 30 minutes ● Serves 6 to 8.

For the stuffing
30 to 40 spinach leaves
100 grams (4 oz.) crumbled paneer
½ teaspoon green chillies
salt to taste

For the dough
1 teacup plain flour
2 teaspoons butter
½ teaspoon salt

For the cream sauce
1 teacup milk
2 tablespoons plain flour
100 grams (4 oz.) fresh cream
2 tablespoons grated cheese
2 tablespoons butter
salt and pepper to taste

For the tomato gravy (optional)
½ kg (1⅛ lb.) red, ripe tomatoes, cut into big pieces
50 grams (2 oz.) fresh cream
3 to 4 teaspoons sugar
½ teaspoon oregano or
  1 teaspoon fresh chopped tulsi leaves
1 pinch ajwain
½ teaspoon chilli powder
salt to taste

For the baking
2 tablespoons grated cheese

For the stuffing
1. Steam the spinach leaves. Squeeze out the water.
2. Chop the spinach leaves finely and mix with the paneer, green chillies and salt.

For the dough
Mix the flour, butter and salt. Add water and make a semi-stiff dough.

For the cream sauce
1. Heat the butter, add the flour and fry for ½ minute.
2. Add the milk and ½ teacup of water and cook until the sauce becomes thick.
3. Add the cheese, cream, salt and pepper.

For the tomato gravy
1. Boil the tomatoes without any water. Blend in a liquidiser and strain.
2. Add the sugar, oregano, ajwain, chilli powder and salt and boil for 10 minutes on a slow flame.
3. Add the cream.

How to proceed
1. Separate the dough into 15 balls and roll out into thin puris. Spread some spinach filling in each puri and close.
2. Put plenty of water to boil and add 1 tablespoon of oil. Boil batches of the puris (tartillini) for ½ minute. Drain and keep aside in a little water.
3. In a greased baking dish, spread a little cream sauce and some tartillini. If you like, sprinkle a little tomato gravy. Make more layers in this manner. Sprinkle the balance cheese and bake in a hot oven at 230°C (450°F) for 10 minutes..

★ Serve hot.

BAKED SPINACH PANCAKES IN TOMATO GRAVY

Lovely spinach pancakes served with spicy tomato gravy.
Preparation time: 20 minutes • Cooking time: 30 minutes • Serves 6 to 8.

For the pancakes
1 teacup chopped spinach
100 grams (4 oz.) plain flour
3 teaspoons ghee
½ teaspoon salt
1 teacup milk

For the vegetables
3 teacups mixed boiled
  vegetables (french beans,
  carrots, green peas, potatoes,
  cauliflower), finely chopped
1 chopped onion
1 teaspoon chilli powder
1 tablespoon butter *or* ghee

For the tomato gravy
750 grams (1⅝ lb.) tomatoes,
  chopped
1 chopped onion
2 cloves crushed garlic
2 teaspoons sugar (approx.)
1 teaspoon chilli powder
2 tablespoons oil

For the baking
2 tablespoons fresh cream
2 tablespoons grated cheese

For the pancakes
1. Put the spinach to cook with very little water.
2. When cooked, blend in a liquidiser.
3. Mix the flour, ghee, salt and milk. Add half of the spinach purée and mix well.
4. Prepare pancakes on a non-stick frying pan using a little ghee.

For the vegetables
1. Heat the butter and fry the onion for 1 minute.
2. Add the remaining ingredients along with the remaining spinach purée.

For the tomato gravy
1. Heat the oil and fry the onion and garlic for 1 minute.
2. Add the tomatoes, sugar and chilli powder and cook until soft. Blend in a liquidiser.

How to proceed
1. Spread a little tomato gravy at the bottom of a greased baking dish. Put a pancake in the dish, spread some vegetables and a little gravy on top. Repeat and build up layers of pancakes, vegetables and gravy in this manner.
2. Finally, cover with the cream and top with grated cheese.
3. Bake in a hot oven at 200°C (400°F) for 20 minutes.

★ Serve hot.

BAKED PANCAKES IN PAPRIKA SAUCE

You will enjoy these pancakes with spicy sauce.
Preparation time: 20 minutes ● Cooking time: 30 minutes ● Serves 6 to 8.

For the pancakes
100 grams (4 oz.) plain flour
240 to 270 ml. (8 to 9 fl.oz.) milk
1   egg (optional)
a pinch salt
2   to 3 teaspoons melted butter *or*
    ghee

For the paprika sauce and stuffing
1½ teacups milk
3   tablespoons butter
2   level tablespoons cornflour
½   teaspoon chilli powder
1   chopped onion
2   teacups mixed boiled
     vegetables (french beans,
     carrots, cauliflower, potatoes),
     finely chopped
salt to taste

For the baking
100 grams (4 oz.) fresh cream
2   tablespoons thick curds
6   tablespoons grated cheese
salt to taste

For decoration
potato wafers

For the pancakes
1. Mix the flour, milk, egg and salt into a
   batter. Keep aside for 20 minutes.
2. Prepare small pancakes in a frying pan,
   using a little butter. Use a non-stick frying
   pan if not using egg.

For the paprika sauce and stuffing
1. Heat the butter and fry the onion till
   golden in colour.
2. Add the cornflour and fry again for at
   least 2 minutes.
3. Add the chilli powder and fry again for a
   few seconds.
4. Add the milk and go on stirring and
   cooking until the mixture is thick.
5. Add the boiled vegetables and salt.

How to proceed
1. Beat the cream until thick.
2. Add the curds, salt and half of the cheese.
   Mix well.
3. Fill the pancakes with the vegetable
   mixture.
4. Arrange all the pancakes on a greased
   baking dish.
5. Pour the cream on top, sprinkle the
   remaining cheese and bake in a hot oven
   at 230°C (450°F) for 15 minutes.

   ★ Surround with potato wafers and serve
     hot.

BAKED SPINACH ROLLS

Spicy vegetables rolled in spinach leaves make a delicious baked dish.
Preparation time: 20 minutes • Cooking time: 20 minutes • Serves 6 to 8.

For the stuffing
2 teacups mixed boiled
   vegetables (french beans,
   carrots, green peas, potatoes,
   cauliflower), finely chopped
1 boiled potato
1 chopped onion
1 chopped green chilli
1 teaspoon chilli powder
1 tablespoon chopped coriander
3 tablespoons white sauce,
   page 123
1 tablespoon butter
salt to taste

Other ingredients
20 large spinach leaves
4 teacups white sauce, *page 123*
3 to 4 tablespoons cooking
   cheese

For the stuffing
1. Mash the potato.
2. Heat the butter and fry the onion for
   1 minute. Add the green chilli and fry
   again for ½ minute.
3. Add the mashed potato, vegetables, chilli
   powder, coriander, white sauce and salt
   and cook for 2 minutes.

How to proceed
1. Drop the spinach leaves into salted hot
   water. After 5 minutes, drain.
2. Put a little stuffing in each leaf and roll up.
3. Spread a little white sauce on a greased
   baking tray. Arrange the rolls, pour the
   balance white sauce on top, sprinkle the
   cheese and bake in a hot oven at 230°C
   (450°F) for 10 minutes.

   ★ Serve hot.

Note: Instead of spinach leaves, you can
also use cabbage leaves.

FRENCH STYLE BAKED PANCAKES

Very french, very tasty.
Preparation time: 20 minutes ● Cooking time: 30 minutes ● Serves 6 to 8.

For the pancakes
100 grams (4 oz.) plain flour
240 to 270 ml. (8 to 9 fl.oz.) milk
2 to 3 teaspoons melted butter *or* ghee
1 egg (optional)
a pinch salt
a little ghee for frying

For the stuffing
3 teacups spinach (chopped)
1 chopped onion
1 tablespoon fresh cream
1 chopped chilli
1 tablespoon ghee
salt to taste

For the tomato sauce
1 kg. (2¼ lb.) tomatoes, cut into big pieces
¾ teaspoon chilli powder
3 to 4 teaspoons sugar
2 tablespoons fresh cream
2 tablespoons tomato ketchup
salt to taste

For the baking
2 tablespoons fresh cream
4 tablespoons grated cheese

For the pancakes
1. Mix the flour, milk, butter, egg and salt into a batter. Keep aside for 20 minutes.
2. Prepare small pancakes in a frying pan, using a little ghee. Use a non-stick frying pan if not using egg.

For the stuffing
1. Heat the ghee and fry the onion for ½ minute.
2. Boil the spinach in very little water. Drain.
3. Add the remaining ingredients and mix.

For the tomato sauce
1. Boil the tomatoes without any water. When cooked, blend in a liquidiser and strain.
2. Add the chilli powder, sugar and salt and boil for 10 minutes on a slow fire.
3. Add the cream and ketchup.

How to proceed
1. Put some stuffing in the centre of each pancake, spread a little tomato sauce over it and roll up.
2. Spread a little tomato sauce at the bottom of the baking dish and arrange the pancakes over it.
3. When you want to bake, pour the balance tomato sauce over it.
4. Spread the fresh cream on top, sprinkle the cheese and bake in a hot oven at 230°C (450°F) for 5 to 10 minutes.

★ Serve hot.

VEGETABLE BALLS IN TOMATO SAUCE

Simple yet different.
Preparation time: 20 minutes ● Cooking time: 30 minutes ● Serves 6.

For the vegetable balls
2 teacups mixed boiled
    vegetables (french beans,
    carrots, green peas, potatoes,
    cauliflower), finely chopped
2 boiled and mashed potatoes
2 tablespoons plain flour
4 chopped green chillies
½ teaspoon garam masala
1 tablespoon cashewnut pieces
5 to 6 raisins cut into small pieces
2 teaspoons lemon juice
1 tablespoon chopped coriander
salt to taste

For frying the vegetable balls
batter of ½ teacup plain flour and
    1 teacup water
bread crumbs
oil for deep frying

For the tomato sauce
1 kg. (2¼ lb.) tomatoes, cut into
    big pieces
¾ teaspoon chilli powder
3 to 4 tablespoons sugar
2 tablespoons fresh cream
2 tablespoons tomato ketchup
salt to taste

For the baking (optional)
2 teaspoons fresh cream
3 tablespoons grated cheese

For the vegetable balls
1. Mix the ingredients for the balls and
   shape into small balls.
2. Dip the balls in the batter, roll into bread
   crumbs and deep fry in oil.

For the tomato sauce
1. Boil the tomatoes without any water.
   When cooked, blend in a liquidiser and
   strain.
2. Add the chilli powder, sugar and salt and
   boil for 10 minutes on a slow flame.
3. Add the cream and ketchup.

How to proceed
1. Arrange the balls in a serving tray and
   serve with the hot sauce.
2. If you wish to serve baked, arrange the
   balls in a baking tray, pour the hot sauce
   on top, spread the cream and sprinkle the
   cheese on top. Bake in a hot oven at 230°C
   (450°F) for 5 minutes.

★ Serve hot.

BAKED VEGETABLES IN SPINACH SAUCE

Tasty and nourishing.

Preparation time: 20 minutes ● Cooking time: 30 minutes ● Serves 6 to 8.

For the vegetables
3 teacups mixed boiled
    vegetables (french beans,
    carrots, green peas, cauliflower,
    potatoes)
1 chopped onion
1 teaspoon chilli powder
1 tablespoon butter
salt to taste

For the spinach sauce
2 teacups chopped spinach
200 grams (7 oz.) fresh cream
1 teacup white sauce, *page 123*
salt and pepper to taste

For the baking
5 to 6 tablespoons grated cheese

For the vegetables
1. Heat the butter and fry the onion for
   1 minute.
2. Add the vegetables and cook for
   1 minute.
3. Add the chilli powder and salt.

For the spinach sauce
1. Cook the spinach with very little water. If
   you like, add a pinch of soda bi-carb.
2. When cooked, blend in a liquidiser.
   Strain.
3. Beat the cream, add the spinach purée,
   white sauce, salt and pepper and mix
   well.

How to proceed
1. Mix the vegetables, sauce and half the
   cheese.
2. Spread on a greased baking dish, sprinkle
   the balance cheese on top and bake in a
   hot oven at 230°C (450°F) for 15 to 20
   minutes.

   ★ Serve hot.

BAKED VEGETABLES IN TOMATO SAUCE

A spicy and tasty dish which your guests will enjoy.
Preparation time: 20 minutes ● Cooking time: 30 minutes ● Serves 6 to 8.

2 boiled potatoes
1 brinjal
2 teacups boiled mixed vegetables (french beans, carrots, green peas)
1 chopped onion
1 tablespoon plain flour
1 teacup tomato ketchup
½ teaspoon chilli powder
1 teaspoon chilli sauce (optional)
1 to 2 teaspoons sugar
1½ tablespoons butter
salt to taste
ghee for deep frying

For the topping
1½ teacups white sauce, *page 123*
4 tablespoons grated cheese
a little butter

1. Slice the potatoes and deep fry in ghee.
2. Slice the brinjals and deep fry in ghee.
3. Heat the butter and fry the onion for 1 minute.
4. Add the flour and fry again for ½ minute.
5. Add the tomato ketchup, 1 teacup of water, chilli powder, chilli sauce, sugar and salt and mix well.
6. Add the mixed vegetables and cook for a little while.

How to proceed
1. Make a layer of half of the potatoes and brinjals in a greased baking dish.
2. Spread the vegetable mixture on top and make a second layer of the balance potatoes and brinjals.
3. Next, spread the white sauce and sprinkle the grated cheese on top.
4. Dot with butter and bake in a hot oven at 230°C (450°F) for 20 minutes.

★ Serve hot.

CORN AND SPINACH RICE

Unusual, delicious and nourishing.
Preparation time: 45 minutes ● Cooking time: 20 minutes ● Serves 6.

For the rice
3 teacups cooked rice
1 tablespoon butter
½ teacup milk
salt to taste

For the corn
2 teacups cooked and crushed
   corn
½ teacup milk
1 tablespoon butter
1 chopped onion
1 chopped green chilli
1 tablespoon fresh cream
½ teaspoon sugar
salt to taste

For the spinach
3 teacups chopped spinach
1 chopped onion
1 chopped green chilli
1 tablespoon ghee
a pinch soda bi-carb
salt to taste

For the tomato sauce
4 tomatoes
3 cloves crushed garlic
1 tablespoon oil
1 chopped onion
¾ teaspoon chilli powder
1 teaspoon chopped tulsi leaves
   or oregano
1 teaspoon sugar (approx.)
1 tablespoon fresh cream
salt to taste

For the rice
Melt the butter, add the rice, milk and salt
and cook for 1 minute.

For the corn
1. Heat the butter and fry the onion for
   1 minute. Add the green chilli and fry
   again for a few seconds.
2. Add the corn, milk, cream, sugar and salt
   and cook for 1 minute.

For the spinach
1. Heat the ghee and fry the onion for
   1 minute. Add the green chilli and fry
   again for a little while.
2. Add the spinach, soda bi-carb and salt
   and cook until soft.

For the tomato sauce
1. Put the tomatoes in hot water. After
   10 minutes, remove the skin and chop.
2. Heat the oil and fry the onion for
   1 minute. Add the crushed garlic and fry
   again for a little while.
3. Add the tomatoes, chilli powder, tulsi
   leaves, sugar and salt.
4. Cook on a slow flame for at least 15
   minutes.
5. Add the cream.

For the mushroom sauce
1. Heat the butter and fry the onion for
   1 minute. Add the green chilli and
   mushrooms and fry for at least 3 to
   4 minutes.
2. Add the water or wine and cook again for
   2 to 3 minutes.
3. Add the white sauce, lemon juice, cheese
   and salt.

For the mushroom sauce

1 teacup chopped mushrooms
1 chopped green chilli
1 chopped onion
1 tablespoon butter
¾ teacup water *or* white wine
1 teacup thin white sauce,
   page 123
1 teaspoon lemon juice
2 tablespoons grated cheese
salt to taste

How to proceed

1. Spread the spinach at the bottom of a greased jelly mould.
2. Spread the corn on the spinach.
3. Spread the rice on top. Press well and cover.
4. Bake in a hot oven at 200°C (400°F) for 10 minutes.
5. Invert on a plate. Serve hot with tomato or mushroom sauce.

SPINACH DUMPLINGS IN TOMATO GRAVY

PICTURE ON PAGE 38

An adaptation of the Italian malfatti.
Preparation time: 15 minutes ● Cooking time: 30 minutes ● Serves 6.

For the dumplings

4 teacups finely chopped spinach leaves
1 teacup crumbled paneer
2 pinches nutmeg powder
½ teaspoon chopped green chillies
6 teaspoons plain flour
2 pinches baking powder
salt to taste

For the tomato gravy

1 kg. (2¼ lb.) tomatoes
3 to 4 teaspoons sugar
½ teaspoon oregano *or*
   1 teaspoon fresh chopped tulsi leaves
1 pinch ajwain *or* ¼ teaspoon oregano
½ teaspoon chilli powder
100 grams (4 oz.) fresh cream
2 tablespoons grated cheese
salt to taste

For the dumplings

1. Steam the spinach leaves for 5 minutes. Squeeze out the water.
2. Mix all the ingredients and shape into small rounds.
3. Steam for 4 to 5 minutes.

For the tomato gravy

1. Boil the tomatoes without any water. Blend in a mixer and strain.
2. Add the sugar, oregano, ajwain, chilli powder and salt and boil for a few minutes.
3. Add half the cream.

How to proceed

1. Immerse the dumplings in hot water for a few seconds.
2. Remove and arrange on a serving dish.
3. Just before serving, pour the boiling tomato gravy over the dumplings. Spread the balance cream on top. Top with cheese. If you wish bake in a hot oven at 200°C (400°F) for about 5 minutes.

★ Serve hot.

POTATO PEAS PATTIES IN TOMATO SAUCE

Children will love this dish.
Preparation time: 30 minutes ● Cooking time: 30 minutes ● Serves 6 to 8.

For the potato patties

1 kg. (2¼ lb.) boiled and grated potatoes ⎫
2 tablespoons cornflour ⎪ to be
juice of ½ lemon ⎬ mixed
1 chopped green chilli ⎪ into a
½ teaspoon sugar ⎭ dough

salt to taste
2 teacups boiled green peas
1 tablespoon thick cream
½ teaspoon sugar
salt to taste

To be ground into a paste (for the patties)

¾ teacup chopped coriander
5 green chillies
1 tablespoon grated fresh coconut
½ teaspoon sugar
1 teaspoon salt

For frying the patties

batter of ½ teacup plain flour and 1 teacup water
bread crumbs
oil for deep frying

For the tomato sauce

1 kg. (2¼ lb.) tomatoes, cut into big pieces
¾ teaspoon chilli powder
3 to 4 teaspoons sugar
2 tablespoons fresh cream
2 tablespoons tomato ketchup
salt to taste

For serving

grated cheese

For the potato patties

1. Mix the green peas, paste, cream, sugar and salt.
2. Make small balls from the potato dough. Flatten the balls.
3. Place a little mixture on each potato round and close to form patties.
4. Dip the patties in the batter, roll into bread crumbs and deep fry in oil.

For the tomato sauce

1. Boil the tomatoes without any water. When cooked, blend in a liquidiser and strain.
2. Add the chilli powder, sugar and salt and boil for 10 minutes on a slow flame.
3. Add the cream and ketchup.

How to proceed

1. Place the patties on a serving dish and pour the hot tomato gravy over them. Sprinkle the grated cheese on top and serve hot.
2. Alternatively, bake in a hot oven at 200°C (400°F) for a few minutes before serving.

STUFFED POTATO PICTURE ON PAGE 112

A nourishing meal which children will love.
You may choose any one of the three fillings or their combinations as you wish.
Preparation time: 10 minutes ● Cooking time: 50 minutes ● Serves 6.

6 large potatoes

For the bean filling (for 6 potatoes)
1 small can (225 grams) baked beans
1 small onion, finely chopped
1 finely chopped green chilli
1 tablespoon oil *or* butter
salt and pepper to taste
1 teacup white sauce, *page 123* and 4 tablespoons grated cheese for topping

For the corn filling (for 6 potatoes)
1 teacup cooked corn
1 small onion, finely chopped
1 finely chopped green chilli
3 tablespoons white sauce, *page 123*
1 tablespoon butter
salt and pepper to taste
1 teacup white sauce, *page 123* and 4 tablespoons grated cheese for topping

For the cream cheese filling (for 6 potatoes)
1 teacup fresh thick curds
1 tablespoon fresh cream
1 finely chopped green chilli
salt to taste

1. Brush the potatoes with oil.
2. Wrap in an aluminium foil and bake in a hot oven at 200°C (400°F) till tender (about 30 minutes)
3. Cool and split horizontally.
4. Scoop the potato halves a little so that a slight depression is formed for the filling.

For the bean filling
1. Heat the oil and fry the onion for ½ minute.
2. Add the green chilli and fry again for a few seconds.
3. Add the beans and cook for 2 minutes.
4. Add salt and pepper.

For the corn filling
1. Heat the butter and fry the onion for ½ minute.
2. Add the green chilli and fry again for a few seconds.
3. Add the corn, white sauce, salt and pepper and cook for 1 minute.

For the cream cheese filling
1. Mix all the ingredients thoroughly.
2. Chill.

How to proceed
1. Fill each potato half with the filling of your choice (the quantities of each filling are given for six potatoes and should be adjusted as required).
2. If using cream cheese filling, serve the hot potatoes with the cold cream cheese.
3. If using the bean or corn filling, grill under an oven before serving. Alternatively, bake in a hot oven at 200°C (400°F) for 10 minutes.

★ Serve hot.

SPICY PANCAKES PICTURE ON FACING PAGE

A delicious and colourful dish.
Preparation time: 20 minutes ● Cooking time: 40 minutes ● Serves 6 to 8.

For the pancakes
100 grams (4 oz.) plain flour
240 to 270 ml. (8 to 9 fl.oz.) milk
2 to 3 teaspoons melted butter *or* ghee
1 egg (optional)
a pinch salt

For the stuffing
1 chopped onion
3 teacups mixed boiled vegetables (french beans, carrots, green peas, potatoes, cauliflower), finely chopped
2 boiled and mashed potatoes
1 teaspoon chilli powder
1 tablespoon butter
salt to taste

For the baking
3 teacups white sauce, *page 123*
1 teacup tomato ketchup
3 tablespoons grated cheese
1 small can (225 grams) baked beans
a little butter
salt to taste

For the pancakes
1. Mix the flour, milk, butter, egg and salt into a batter. Keep aside for 20 minutes.
2. Prepare small pancakes in a frying pan using a little butter. Use a non-stick frying pan if not using egg.

For the stuffing
1. Heat the butter and fry the onion until golden.
2. Add the remaining ingredients and cook for 1 minute.

How to proceed
1. Spread a little white sauce in a greased baking dish.
2. Fill each pancake with a little stuffing, then spread 1 tablespoon of tomato ketchup and close. Repeat with the remaining pancakes and stuffing. Place the stuffed pancakes in the dish.
3. Spread the remaining white sauce on top and then the balance tomato ketchup. Sprinkle the cheese and make a border of baked beans. Dot with butter.
4. Bake in a hot oven at 230°C (450°F) for 20 minutes.

★ Serve hot.

1. FRENCH ONION SOUP, *Page 21*
2. SPICY PANCAKES, *Above*

VI. Chinese Dishes

MEE HOON PICTURE ON FACING PAGE

A delicious dish of noodles and vegetables which you can eat as a snack or as a meal.
Preparation time: 15 minutes ● Cooking time: 15 minutes ● Serves 4 to 6.

1 packet (100 grams) chow noodles
1 carrot, cut into long strips
1 sliced onion
1 sliced cucumber
1 capsicum, sliced lengthwise
a few spinach stems
½ teaspoon Ajinomoto powder
½ teaspoon sugar
3 tablespoons refined oil
salt to taste

To be ground into a paste
4 cloves garlic
4 red chillies

To serve
2 teaspoons chilli oil, *page 122*
cucumber slices
chopped spring onions

For the noodles
1. Boil the noodles.
2. Heat 1½ tablespoons of oil and fry the boiled noodles.

How to proceed
1. Heat the remaining 1½ tablespoons of oil and fry the paste for a few minutes.
2. Add the carrot, onion, cucumber, capsicum, spinach stems and Ajinomoto powder and fry again for 2 minutes.
3. Add the fried vegetables, sugar and salt to the fried noodles and mix well.
4. Top with the chilli oil, surround with cucumber slices, sprinkle chopped spring onions on top and serve hot.

1. SIZZLING WONTONS WITH SWEET AND SOUR VEGETABLES, *Page 60*
2. CRISPY RICE SOUP, *Page 58*
3. MEE HOON, *Above*

CRISPY RICE SOUP PICTURE ON PAGE 56

The crackle of the rice when added to the soup gives a sizzling start to your meal.
Preparation time: 10 minutes ● Cooking time: 10 minutes ● Serves 6.

1 teacup cauliflower, cut into big pieces
2 tablespoons chopped lettuce leaves
2 sliced carrots
1 tablespoon chopped celery
2 tablespoons chopped spring onions without leaves
1 medium sized firm tomato, cut into small pieces
4 to 5 tablespoons cooked and dried rice
¼ teaspoon Ajinomoto powder
2 tablespoons refined oil
refined oil for deep frying
salt to taste

1. Heat the oil on a high flame and add the cauliflower, carrot, celery, spring onions, Ajinomoto powder and cook for 3 to 4 minutes.
2. Add 6 teacups of hot water, the tomato pieces, lettuce and salt and give one boil.
3. Pour into a large serving bowl.
4. Deep fry the dried rice on a high flame.
5. Just before serving, add the rice.

★ Serve hot with chillies in vinegar and chilli sauce.

CRISPY RICE

Spread the cooked rice in a broad vessel and put in the sun. Cover with a jali (sieve) and keep until the rice is fully dried. Store in an air-tight jar. The dried rice stays for several months without spoiling.

CHILLI GARLIC NOODLES

A top favourite with the chilli lovers.
Preparation time: 10 minutes ● Cooking time: 5 minutes ● Serves 4 to 6.

3 teacups boiled noodles
a few spring onion leaves
¼ teaspoon Ajinomoto powder
½ teacup chilli garlic sauce, page 122
1 tablespoon chilli oil, page 122
2 tablespoons refined oil

1. Heat the refined oil thoroughly.
2. Add the spring onion leaves, Ajinomoto powder, noodles and garlic sauce and cook on a high flame for 3 to 4 minutes.
3. Pour the chilli oil on top and toss.

★ Serve hot.

ONION PANCAKES

A popular starter for the meal.
Preparation time: 10 minutes • Cooking time: 20 minutes • Makes 20 to
25 small pieces.

For the pancakes
½ teacup cornflour
½ teacup plain flour
½ teacup milk
½ teacup water
a pinch salt
2 teaspoons melted butter *or*
ghee *or* oil

For the filling
3 teacups chopped spring onions
with leaves
1 tablespoon refined oil
½ teaspoon Ajinomoto powder
a pinch of sugar
salt to taste

For the pancakes
1. Mix all the ingredients into a batter.
2. Spread 1 tablespoon of the batter onto a non-stick frying pan and cook on both sides with a little oil. Repeat for the remaining batter.

For the filling
1. Heat the oil on a high flame, add the onions and Ajinomoto powder and cook for 2 minutes.
2. Add the sugar and salt and remove from the gas.
3. Drain away the liquid, if any.

How to proceed
1. Spread 1 tablespoon of the filling on each pancake, fold and if desired, seal the edges by applying a little of the pancake mixture.
2. Deep fry in oil.

★ Cut into pieces and serve hot.

Variation: COCONUT PANCAKES You can make coconut pancakes in the same manner using a filling of a mixture of 1 teacup of grated fresh coconut, ½ teacup of sugar and 1 drop of rose or vanilla essence (optional) instead of the above filling. And after filling this mixture into the pancakes, sprinkle sesame seeds on top before frying.

SIZZLING WONTONS WITH SWEET AND SOUR VEGETABLES PICTURE ON PAGE 56

A crispy Chinese sizzler combining delicious wontons with popular sweet and sour vegetables.

Preparation time: 30 minutes ● Cooking time: 30 minutes ● Serves 4 to 6.

For the dough (wontons)
1½ teacups plain flour
½ teaspoon salt
3 teaspoons refined oil

For the dough (wontons)
1. Mix all the ingredients and add enough water to make a stiff dough.
2. Roll out into very thin circles.

For the stuffing (wontons)
1 teacup boiled noodles
2 teacups shredded cabbage
2 sliced onions
1 grated carrot
1 teacup bean sprouts
½ teaspoon Ajinomoto powder
1 teaspoon soya sauce
2 tablespoons refined oil
refined oil for deep frying
salt to taste

For the stuffing (wontons)
1. Heat 2 tablespoons of oil on a high flame.
2. Add the cabbage, onions, carrot, bean sprouts and Ajinomoto powder and cook for 3 minutes.
3. Add the noodles, soya sauce and salt.

How to proceed (wontons)
1. Put a little stuffing on each dough circle and fold over to make a semi circle. Bring the ends together and press.
2. Repeat with the remaining dough and stuffing.
3. Deep fry in oil.

For the sweet and sour vegetables
100 grams (4 oz.) french beans
4 sticks celery
100 grams (4 oz.) carrots
100 grams (4 oz.) onions
100 grams (4 oz.) cauliflower
100 grams (4 oz.) cabbage
100 grams (4 oz.) cucumber
100 grams (4 oz.) capsicum
½ teaspoon Ajinomoto powder
4 tablespoons refined oil
salt to taste

For the sweet and sour vegetables
1. Cut the french beans and celery into 25 mm. (1") pieces.
2. Slice the carrots and onions.
3. Cut the rest of the vegetables into flat pieces.
4. Heat the oil on a high flame, add the vegetables and Ajinomoto powder and cook for 2 to 3 minutes. Add salt.

For the sweet and sour sauce
½ teacup brown vinegar
½ teacup sugar
¾ teacup water
2 tablespoons cornflour
1 tablespoon soya sauce
4 tablespoons tomato ketchup

For serving
chillies in vinegar
chilli sauce

For the sweet and sour sauce
1. Mix all the ingredients and put to boil.
2. Go on cooking and stirring until the sauce becomes thick.

How to proceed
1. Heat the sizzler tray (thick cast iron tray) thoroughly.
2. Spread the vegetables on the sides and put the wontons in the centre.
3. Pour the sauce on top of the vegetables and wontons and sizzle on the gas or in the oven.

★ Serve hot with chillies in vinegar and chilli sauce.

PANEER IN MANCHURIAN SAUCE

A combination of paneer and Manchurian sauce.
Preparation time: 15 minutes ● Cooking time: 10 minutes ● Serves 4 to 6.

2 teacups sliced paneer
1 tablespoon chopped green chillies
1 tablespoon chopped garlic
1 tablespoon chopped ginger
¼ teaspoon Ajinomoto powder
1 level tablespoon cornflour
4 teaspoons soya sauce
2 teaspoons chilli-garlic sauce, *page 122*
2 pinches sugar
1 tablespoon refined oil
refined oil for frying

1. Fry the paneer lightly in oil.
2. Heat 1 tablespoon of oil in a separate vessel and fry the chillies, garlic and ginger for a few minutes. Add the Ajinomoto powder.
3. Mix the cornflour in 1½ teacups of water and add to the mixture.
4. Add the soya sauce, chilli-garlic sauce and sugar and cook until the mixture becomes thick.
5. Add the paneer and cook for 1 minute.

★ Serve hot.

Variation: POTATOES IN MANCHURIAN SAUCE Omit the first step and instead of paneer use 20 very small boiled and fried potatoes

SZECHWAN RICE

A tasty rice with the characteristic Szechwan taste.
Preparation time: 25 minutes ● Cooking time: 10 minutes ● Serves 6.

1½ teacups uncooked rice
1   teacup grated cabbage
1   teacup grated carrots
½   teaspoon Ajinomoto powder
1   tablespoon soya sauce
1   tablespoon sliced red chillies,
    soaked in vinegar
2   tablespoons refined oil
salt to taste

1. Boil the rice. Each grain of the cooked rice should be separate. Cool for at least 2 hours.
2. Heat the oil on a high flame and fry the cabbage and carrots with Ajinomoto powder for 2 minutes.
3. Add the rice, red chillies, soya sauce and salt and mix well.

★ Serve hot.

STACKED ENCHILADAS

The favourite Mexican dish cooked in a different way.
Preparation time: 20 minutes ● Cooking time: 35 minutes ● Serves 6 to 8.

For the dough
2   teacups plain flour
1   teacup whole wheat flour
4   teaspoons oil
½ teaspoon salt
oil for deep frying

To be mixed into a filling
2   teacups chopped paneer
1   chopped onion
1   chopped green chilli
salt to taste

For the baking
hot sauce, *page 69*
100 grams (4 oz.) fresh cream
juice of 1 lemon
100 grams (4 oz.) grated cooking
     cheese
salt to taste

For serving
chopped spring onions (optional)

For the dough
Mix all the ingredients and make a dough by
adding water. Roll out the dough into small
circles with the help of plain flour. Prick
lightly with a fork. Deep fry lightly in oil.

How to proceed
1. Divide the tortillas into three batches for
   making three layers.
2. Arrange one layer on a plate, sprinkle a
   little filling and pour hot sauce on top.
3. Now arrange the second layer and
   similarly sprinkle some filling and hot
   sauce on top.
4. Repeat with the third layer in this manner.
5. Mix the cream, lemon juice and salt and
   pour on top.
6. Sprinkle the cheese and bake in a hot
   oven at 230°C (450°F) for 10 to 15 minutes.
7. If you like, sprinkle lots of spring onions
   on top before serving.

★ Serve hot.

MEXICAN PIZZA PICTURE ON FACING PAGE

A tasty, easy to make pizza.
Preparation time: 20 minutes ● Cooking time: 30 minutes ● Serves 6 to 8.

For the dough (alternative 1)
2 teacups plain flour
1 teacup whole wheat flour
4 teaspoons oil
½ teaspoon salt
oil for deep frying

For the dough (alternative 2)
1½ teacups maize flour
1 teacup plain flour
3 teaspoons oil
¾ teaspoon salt
oil for deep frying

For the topping
1 teacup red kidney beans (rajma)
1 chopped onion
2 tablespoons tomato ketchup
2 tablespoons ghee
2 tablespoons butter
salt to taste

Other ingredients
sour cream *or* fresh cream mixed
   with a little lemon juice
grated cooking cheese
chilli powder
olives
chilli in vinegar (optional)
hot sauce, *page 69*

For the dough
1. Mix the flours. Add the oil and salt and make a soft dough by adding water.
2. Roll out thin rounds about 100 mm. (4") in diameter with the help of plain flour. Prick lightly with a fork.
3. Deep fry in hot oil on both sides on a medium flame until crisp.
4. Store in an air-tight tin.

For the topping.
1. Soak the beans overnight.
2. Next day, cook in a pressure cooker. Drain and mash.
3. Heat the ghee and fry the onion for ½ minute.
4. Add the beans, tomato ketchup, butter and salt and cook for 2 to 3 minutes.
5. When cooked, mash the beans slightly.

How to proceed
1. Put the fried rounds on a plate and spread a little rajma mixture on each.
2. Spread 1 teaspoon of chillies in vinegar, a little hot sauce and a little sour cream on each puri. Then put a few olives and sprinkle cheese and chilli powder on top.
3. Grill for a few minutes.

   ★ Serve hot.

Note: If you like, use cooked corn instead of kidney beans.

1. MACARONI A LA MEXICANA, *Page 68*
2. MEXICAN PIZZA, *Above*
3. SALSA DIP, *Page 67*

SALSA DIP PICTURE ON PAGE 65

A spicy tomato based dip.
Preparation time: 15 minutes • Cooking time: 5 minutes • Makes 1 cup.

3 tomatoes
2 teaspoons chillies in vinegar
1 small onion, finely chopped
½ teaspoon chilli powder
1 capsicum
2 pinches ajwain
1 tablespoon oil
½ teaspoon sugar
½ teaspoon salt

1. Put the tomatoes in hot water for about 10 minutes. Remove the skin and chop.
2. Pierce the capsicum with a fork and hold over the flame until the skin blackens. Remove from the heat, rub off the burnt skin and chop.
3. Heat the oil and fry the onion for ½ minute. Add the remaining ingredients and cook for 3 to 4 minutes.

★ Serve with tortilla chips.

TACO SALAD PICTURE ON PAGE 27

A colourful, quick, tasty salad.
Preparation time: 10 minutes • No cooking • Serves 6.

1 recipe salsa dip, *see above*
1 head lettuce
2 capsicums
4 to 5 spring onions
2 tomatoes
1 teacup boiled red kidney beans (rajma)
2 teacups corn chips

1. Chop the lettuce coarsely.
2. Chop the spring onions with a few leaves.
3. Cut the capsicum into big pieces.
4. Cut the tomatoes into small pieces.
5. Put the lettuce, onions and capsicum into cold water for 10 minutes. Remove from the water, add the tomatoes and beans and put in the refrigerator.

How to serve
Put the salad in a big bowl, surround with corn chips, spread 3 to 4 tablespoons of salsa dip on top and serve.

1. ORANGE ICE-CREAM, *Page 71*
2. HOT FUDGE SUNDAE, *Page 73*
3. BRANDY SNAP CUPS WITH VANILLA ICE-CREAM AND HONEY SAUCE, *Page 77*

MACARONI A LA MEXICANA PICTURE ON PAGE 65

Macaroni prepared in an unusual way based on Mexican style cooking.
Preparation time: 25 minutes ● Cooking time: 40 minutes ● Serves 6 to 8.

For the cheese balls
200 grams (7 oz.) paneer
3 tablespoons plain flour
1 tablespoon chopped coriander
2 chopped green chillies
¼ teaspoon soda bi-carb
salt to taste
oil for deep frying

For the macaroni
2 teacups cooked macaroni
1 kg. (2¼ lb.) tomatoes
1 chopped onion
1 chopped capsicum
3 cloves crushed garlic
1 teaspoon chilli powder
2 teaspoon sugar
2 tablespoons oil
salt to taste

For the kidney bean layer
¾ teacup red kidney beans (rajma)
1 chopped onion
1 tablespoon butter
1 tablespoon ghee
1 teaspoon chilli powder
4 tablespoons tomato ketchup
salt to taste

For the baking
100 grams (4 oz.) fresh cream
2 teaspoons lemon juice
6 tablespoons cooking cheese
½ teaspoon salt
a dash chilli powder

For the cheese balls
Mix all the ingredients. Shape into round
balls and deep fry in oil.

For the macaroni
1. Put the tomatoes in hot water for
   10 minutes. Remove the skin and chop.
2. Heat the oil and fry the onion for
   1 minute.
3. Add the capsicum, garlic and chilli
   powder and fry again for a little while.
4. Add the tomatoes, sugar and salt and
   cook on a slow flame for at least
   10 minutes.
5. Add the macaroni and mix.

For the kidney bean layer
1. Soak the beans overnight. Next day, cook
   in a pressure cooker. Drain and mash.
2. Heat the butter and ghee and fry the
   onion for a few minutes.
3. Add the beans, chilli powder, tomato
   ketchup and salt and cook for a few
   minutes.

How to proceed
1. Beat the cream. Add the lemon juice, 2
   tablespoons of the cooking cheese and
   the salt.
2. In a greased baking dish, first make a
   layer of the beans. Next, spread the layer
   of the macaroni. Put the cheese balls on
   top. Pour the cream over this. Spread the
   remaining cheese and dust chilli powder
   on top.
3. Bake in a hot oven at 230°C (450°F) for 20
   minutes.

★ Serve hot.

BARRITO

A tasty and filling dish.
Preparation time: 20 minutes ● Cooking time: 1 hour ● Serves 6 to 8.

For the dough
2 teacups plain flour
3 teaspoons oil
½ teaspoon salt

For the stuffing
1 teacup red kidney beans (rajma)
2 chopped onions
2 tablespoons butter
1 tablespoon ghee
4 tablespoons tomato ketchup
1 teaspoon chilli powder
salt to taste

For the hot sauce
1 kg. (2¼ lb.) red tomatoes
6 dry red chillies
1 chopped onion
¼ teaspoon ajwain
3 teaspoons sugar
2 tablespoons oil
salt to taste

Other ingredients
1 teacup chopped spring onions
chopped spring onions and grated
    carrots for decoration

For the baking (optional)
100 grams (4 oz.) sour cream *or*
    fresh cream mixed with juice of
    1 lemon
5 to 6 tablespoons grated cheese

For the dough
1. Mix all the ingredients and make a soft
   dough by adding water. Knead well.
2. Roll out into small chapatis and cook
   lightly on a tawa (griddle).

For the stuffing
1. Soak the beans overnight. Next day, cook
   in a pressure cooker. Drain and mash.
2. Heat the butter and ghee and fry the
   onion for 1 minute.
3. Add the beans, tomato ketchup, chilli
   powder and salt and cook for a little while.
   Mash a little.

For the hot sauce
1. Heat the oil in a vessel and fry the onion
   for 1 minute.
2. Add the tomatoes and the chillies and
   cook till the tomatoes are soft.
3. Blend in a liquidiser and strain.
4. Add the ajwain, sugar and salt and boil for
   a few minutes.

How to proceed
1. Fill each chapati with a little stuffing.
   Spread a little hot sauce and spring
   onions, close and serve.
2. If you so wish, you can also serve barritos
   baked. Arrange on a baking tray and pour
   the remaining hot sauce on top. Pour the
   cream over the hot sauce. Sprinkle the
   cheese and bake in a hot oven at 230°C
   (450°F) for 20 minutes.
3. Serve hot surrounded by chopped spring
   onions and grated carrots.

NACHOS

For the cheese lovers!
Preparation time: a few minutes • Cooking time: a few minutes.

ready corn chips or fried tortillas,
cooking cheese
taco salad, *page 67* , *or* refried red
kidney beans (rajma) and
chillies in vinegar for serving

1. Spread about 12 mm. (½″) layer of cheese
on the fried tortillas.
2. Put below the grill until the cheese melts.
3. Serve with taco salad or with refried
kidney beans and with chopped green
chillies soaked in vinegar for 15 minutes.

VIII. Ice-Creams

COUPE JACQUES

A lovely fruit sundae.
Preparation time: a few minutes • No cooking • Serves 6.

1 teacup mixed fruit pieces (fresh or canned)
6 scoops vanilla ice-cream sweetened whipped cream and grated chocolate for decoration
6 wafer biscuits for serving

1. Arrange alternate layers of fruit and ice-cream in a tall glass.
2. Top with whipped cream and dust with grated chocolate.
3. Serve with wafer biscuits.

Variation 1: STRAWBERRY SUNDAE Use 1 teacup of strawberry slices instead of fruit pieces and top with strawberry sauce, *page 82*, instead of with cream and chocolate.

Variation 2: CHOCOLATE STRAWBERRY SUNDAE Combine 1 teacup of strawberry slices with 6 scoops of chocolate ice-cream and top with strawberry sauce, *page 82*.

ORANGE ICE-CREAM PICTURE ON PAGE 66

For the orange lovers. This tasty ice-cream will melt in your mouth.
Preparation time: 25 minutes • No cooking • Serves 8.

1 can (400 grams) condensed milk
2 bottles orange drink
2½ teacups milk
2 tablespoons orange segments
1 teaspoon lemon juice (optional)
grated chocolate to serve

1. Mix all the ingredients.
2. Check the sweetness and adjust to your liking using sugar or lemon juice.
3. Prepare the ice-cream in an ice-cream churner.
4. Sprinkle plenty of grated chocolate and serve.

STRAWBERRY RIPPLE ICE-CREAM

Attractive and delicious.
Preparation time: 30 minutes ● Cooking time: 15 minutes ● Serves 10.

For the vanilla ice-cream
2 litres (3½ pints) milk
¾ teacup granulated sugar
   (approx.)
3 level tablespoons cornflour
500 grams (1⅛ lb.) fresh cream
8 tablespoons powdered sugar
2 teaspoons vanilla essence

For the vanilla ice-cream
1. To ½ litre of milk, add the granulated sugar and cornflour and mix well.
2. Put to boil and go on stirring all the time. When the mixture becomes thick, add to the rest of the milk. Mix well.
3. Beat the cream with the powdered sugar very lightly. Add to the mixture and mix very well.
4. Add the vanilla essence and mix very well.
5. Check the sweetness and adjust to your liking using sugar or lemon juice.
6. Prepare the ice-cream in an ice-cream churner.

For the strawberry sauce
2 teacups strawberry purée
2 teacups water
16 teaspoons granulated sugar
2 level tablespoons cornflour
2 teaspoons lemon juice
a few drops red colouring

For the strawberry sauce
1. Mix the strawberry purée, water, sugar and cornflour and boil until the mixture becomes thick.
2. Blend in a liquidiser.
3. Add the lemon juice and colouring.

How to proceed
1. Insert the handle of a metal spoon into the centre of the frozen ice-cream upto the full depth of the ice-cream and make a hole. Pour sauce on top of the ice-cream and stir lightly so that the sauce fills the hole.
2. Pull the spoon handle outward from the centre in a continuous ever-increasing circular direction so as to form a continuous annular groove. Spread the sauce lightly so that it fills the groove and gives a ripple effect.
3. At a convenient point near the outer periphery of the ice-cream, remove the spoon handle.

4. Set again in the freezer compartment of a refrigerator.

Variation: CHOCOLATE RIPPLE ICE-CREAM Use chocolate sauce, *page 119,* instead of strawberry sauce and proceed as above.

HOT FUDGE SUNDAE PICTURE ON PAGE 66

The popular all-time favourite.
Preparation time: 25 minutes ● Cooking time: 10 minutes ● Serves 10.

For the ice-cream
2 litres (3½ pints) milk
¾ teacup sugar (approx.)
3 level tablespoons cornflour
400 grams (14 oz.) fresh cream
2 teaspoons vanilla essence

For the fudge sauce
150 grams (5 oz.) plain chocolate
75 grams (3 oz.) sugar
9 tablespoons boiling water
3 tablespoons butter
3 tablespoons golden syrup
2 teaspoons vanilla essence

For topping
roasted almonds
chopped walnuts

For the ice-cream
1. Keep aside a little cold milk and boil the rest of the milk with the sugar for 5 minutes.
2. Mix the cornflour in the balance cold milk and add to the mixture.
3. Boil for 1 minute while stirring all the time. Cool.
4. Beat the cream very lightly, add to the mixture and mix very well.
5. Add the vanilla essence and mix very well.
6. Check the sweetness and adjust to your liking using sugar or lemon juice.
7. Prepare the ice-cream in an ice-cream churner.

For the fudge sauce
1. Grate the chocolate.
2. Heat the sugar, water and butter and cook until the sugar has melted.
3. Add the golden syrup and the grated chocolate.
4. Cook until the chocolate melts completely.
5. Cool a little and add the vanilla essence.

How to serve
Pour a little warm sauce in a long stem glass. Put a little ice-cream, some sauce and again a little ice-cream. Top with roasted almonds or with chopped walnuts.

COCONUT ICE-CREAM

An unusual blend of coconut with ice-cream. Once you have tasted it, you will always ask for more.
Preparation time: 20 minutes • Cooking time: 15 minutes • Serves 10.

1½ litres (2⅝ pints) milk
1   fresh coconut with thick meat
1   can (400 grams) condensed milk
5   to 6 tablespoons sugar
1   teaspoon vanilla essence
2   tablespoons fresh grated coconut and 1 tablespoon sugar for topping

1. Grate the fresh coconut. Divide into 2 equal portions.
2. To one half of the grated coconut, add 4 tablespoons of milk and blend in a mixer.
3. From the other half of the grated coconut, squeeze out coconut milk. Strain through a thin cloth.
4. Heat 3 tablespoons of sugar in a vessel on a slow flame until it melts. Add the remaining milk and boil until the sugar dissolves. Add the remaining sugar and boil for 5 minutes.
5. Mix the blended coconut (step 2), coconut milk (step 3), sweetened milk (step 4), condensed milk and vanilla essence.
6. Check the sweetness and adjust to your liking using sugar or lemon juice.
7. Prepare the ice-cream in an ice-cream churner.

How to serve
1. Heat 2 tablespoons of fresh grated coconut in the oven until slightly pink in colour. Sprinkle on the ice-cream before serving.
2. Alternatively, mix 2 tablespoons of fresh grated coconut and 1 tablespoon of sugar and cook until the sugar caramalises slightly.

★ Serve hot on top of the ice-cream.

1. STRAWBERRY CHEESE PIE, Page 82
2. ALMOND ROCKS, Page 102

BRANDY SNAP CUPS WITH VANILLA ICE-CREAM AND HONEY SAUCE PICTURE ON PAGE 66

You'll snap up this delightful and elegant dish.
Preparation time: 20 minutes ● Cooking time: 35 minutes ● Serves 10.

For the brandy snap cups
60 grams (2 oz.) butter
60 grams (2 oz.) sugar
55 grams (2 oz.) plain flour
2 tablespoons golden syrup
½ teaspoon ginger powder

For the brandy snap cups
1. Sieve the flour and ginger powder together.
2. Heat the butter, sugar and golden syrup on a slow flame till the sugar is fully melted. Switch off the gas.
3. Add the flour mixture and mix well.
4. Put 1 teaspoon of the mixture at a time on a greased tray, leaving a lot of room in between for expansion. Two greased trays will be required in all.
5. Bake in a moderate oven at 180°C (350°F) for 10 to 12 minutes or until golden brown.
6. Remove and cool. After 2 minutes, test to see if you can slip a pallet knife under the snaps. Remove from the trays and shape the warm snaps into tart cups by pressing.
7. When cold, fill the cups with vanilla ice-cream. Top with honey or strawberry sauce, *page 72.*

For the vanilla ice-cream
2 litres (3½ pints) milk
¾ teacup sugar (approx.)
3 level tablespoons cornflour
400 grams (14 oz.) fresh cream
2 teaspoons vanilla essence

For the vanilla ice-cream
1. Keep aside a little cold milk and boil the rest of the milk with the sugar for 5 minutes.
2. Mix the cornflour in the balance cold milk and add to the mixture.
3. Boil for 1 minute while stirring all the time. Cool.
4. Beat the cream very lightly, add to the mixture and mix very well.
5. Add the vanilla essence and mix very well.
6. Check the sweetness and adjust to your liking using sugar or lemon juice.
7. Prepare the ice-cream in an ice-cream churner.

1. SUNSHINE CHEESECAKE, *Page 83*
2. ORANGE AND LEMON GATEAU, *Page 96*

MALAI KULFI

You will be surprised how light and tasty this kulfi is.
Preparation time: 10 minutes ● Cooking time: 20 minutes ● Makes 30 kulfis.

3 litres (5¼ pints) milk
150 grams (5½ oz.) sugar
1 can (400 grams) condensed milk
2 pinches citric acid
½ teaspoon cardamom powder

1. Put the milk to boil and reduce the volume to three-quarters. Add the sugar and boil again for 3 to 4 minutes.
2. Divide into 2 equal parts and keep aside one part. On the other part, sprinkle 1 pinch citric acid. The milk will curdle after a little while. If it does not curdle, add the remaining pinch of citric acid. Beat up the mixture immediately with an egg beater.
3. Add the condensed milk, the remaining boiled milk and the cardamom powder and mix thoroughly. Pour into kulfi moulds and set in the freezer compartment of a refrigerator for 8 to 10 hours.
4. To serve, remove from the refrigerator, dip the moulds into the water, open and slip out the kulfi. Cut into pieces and serve.

CHOCOLATE CHIP ICE-CREAM

Children will love this ice-cream.
Preparation time: 30 minutes ● Cooking time: 10 minutes ● Serves 10.

For preparation in a churner
2 litres (3½ pints) milk
¾ teacup granulated sugar (approx.)
3 level tablespoons cornflour
400 grams (14 oz.) fresh cream
8 tablespoons powdered sugar
2 teaspoons vanilla essence
3 to 4 tablespoons chocolate chips

For preparation in a churner
1. Keep aside a little cold milk. Mix the rest with the granulated sugar and boil for 5 minutes.
2. Mix the cornflour in the balance cold milk. Add to the sweetened milk, give one boil while stirring all the time. Cool.
3. Add the vanilla essence and mix very well.
4. Beat the cream with the powdered sugar very lightly. Add to the mixture and mix very well.
5. Check the sweetness and adjust to your liking using sugar or lemon juice.
6. Add the chocolate chips.
7. Prepare the ice-cream in an ice-cream churner.

Setting time: 45 minutes ● Cooking time: 5 minutes ● Serves 4.

For preparation in the refrigerator
2 teacups milk
200 grams (7 oz.) fresh cream
1 teaspoon cornflour
4 tablespoons sugar
½ teaspoon vanilla essence
2 tablespoons chocolate chips

For preparation in the refrigerator
1. Heat the milk with half the sugar and the cornflour. Boil till the mixture becomes thick. Cool.
2. Beat the cream with the remaining sugar and add to the milk with the vanilla essence.
3. Check the sweetness and adjust to your liking using sugar or lemon juice.
4. Pour the mixture into two ice-cube trays and put to set in the freezer compartment of a refrigerator.
5. After about 45 minutes, add the chocolate chips and mix well. Put to set again in the freezer compartment for at least 15 minutes.

★ Serve immediately.

PEAR ICE-CREAM

This ice-cream is easily prepared in the refrigerator.
Preparation time: a few minutes ● No cooking● Serves: 6 to 8.

500 grams (1⅛ lb.) ripe pears
juice of 1 lemon
½ teacup milk
1 tablespoon kirsch (optional)
400 grams (14 oz.) fresh cream
5 to 6 tablespoons sugar

1. Peel and chop the pears.
2. Blend the pears with the lemon juice, milk, kirsch and 2 tablespoons of the sugar. Chill.
3. Beat the cream and sugar until thick.
4. Add the chilled pear mixture, mix and beat lightly.
5. Pour into freezer tray and put in the freezer compartment of the refrigerator.
6. After about 1 hour, remove the frozen mixture into a chilled bowl and beat with a fork or wooden spoon to break all ice crystals, adding 50 grams thick cream if you like a smoother ice-cream.
7. Put to set again in freezer trays.

   * Serve immediately or store it in a covered box.

IX. Puddings and Pies

FRENCH APPLE TART

This different and juicy apple tart just tastes yummy.
Preparation time: 20 minutes • Cooking time: 30 minutes • Serves 6 to 8.

For the pastry
150 grams (5½ oz.) plain flour
a pinch salt
2 teaspoons powdered sugar
75 grams (2¾ oz.) butter
1 tablespoon powdered
   cashewnuts *or* almonds

For the apple tart
2 · sliced apples
25 grams (1 oz.) butter
30 grams (1 oz.) granulated sugar
½ teaspoon lemon juice
1 teaspoon powdered sugar
a little milk for brushing

To serve
vanilla ice-cream *or* fresh cream

For the pastry
1. Mix the flour, salt and sugar and sieve.
   Rub in the butter and enough water and
   make a soft dough.
2. Mix the powdered nuts thoroughly in the
   dough.
3. Roll out the dough to suit a 225 mm. (9″)
   diameter tray. Prick with a fork all over.

How to proceed
1. Put a baking tray on the gas with the
   butter and granulated sugar. When the
   sugar turns brown in colour, switch off
   the gas and allow it to cool a little.
2. Spread the apple slices on the tray and
   sprinkle the lemon juice and powdered
   sugar.
3. Place the rolled pastry dough over the
   apple slices and brush with a little milk.
   Bake in a moderate oven at 190°C (375°F)
   for 20 to 25 minutes. Turn it upside down.

   ★ Serve with vanilla ice-cream or fresh
     cream.

STRAWBERRY CHEESE PIE PICTURE ON PAGE 75

An elegant, colourful cheesecake which your guests will love.
Preparation time: 20 minutes ● Cooking time: 10 minutes ● Serves 10.

For the crust
6 tablespoons crushed Marie biscuits
4 tablespoons melted butter

For the filling
1 packet (11 grams) gelatine
½ teacup fresh curds
2 tablespoons powdered sugar
1 family pack (½ litre) vanilla ice-cream
a few slices strawberries

For the strawberry sauce
1 teacup strawberry purée
2 teaspoons cornflour
7 teaspoons sugar
1 teaspoon lemon juice
a few drops red colouring

For decoration
100 grams (4 oz.) fresh cream
2 tablespoons powdered sugar

For the crust
1. Mix the biscuits and butter and press the mixture evenly into the bottom of a 175 or 200 mm. (7" or 8") diameter loose bottom tin.
2. Place in the refrigerator until firm.

For the filling
1. Mix the gelatine in ¾ teacup of cold water and warm on a slow flame until it dissolves.
2. Add the gelatine, curds and sugar to the vanilla ice-cream.
3. Place the vessel over warm water and stir until it becomes a smooth mixture.

For the strawberry sauce
1. Mix the strawberry purée, cornflour, sugar and ¾ teacup of water.
2. Put to boil and go on stirring until it becomes a thick sauce.
3. Add the lemon juice and colouring.
4. Chill.

How to proceed
1. Arrange a few sliced strawberries over the crust and pour the filling over it. Put to set in the refrigerator.
2. Beat the cream and sugar until thick.
3. Remove the set pie from the tin and put on serving plate.
4. Pipe the cream with a star nozzle around the edges of the pie.
5. Pour the sauce in the centre. Chill.
6. Cut into slices and serve.

SUNSHINE CHEESECAKE PICTURE ON PAGE 76

A delicious cheesecake served with a rich sauce.
Preparation time: 20 minutes ● Cooking time: 10 minutes ● Serves 8 to 10.

For the crust
8 tablespoons crushed Marie biscuits
6 tablespoons melted butter
25 grams (1 oz.) powdered sugar

For the filling
1 packet (100 grams) pineapple jelly
1 family pack (½ litre) vanilla ice-cream
2 tablespoons fresh curds
2 tablespoons powdered sugar
juice of ½ lemon

For serving
cherry sauce *or* peach sauce
   (see below)

For the crust
1. Mix the butter, biscuits and sugar and press into a 200 or 225 mm. (8" or 9") diameter loose bottom cake or flan tin.
2. Chill until firm or bake in a moderate oven at 180°C (350°F) for 10 to 15 minutes.

How to proceed
1. Dissolve the jelly in 2 teacups of boiling water. Pour the boiling jelly liquid over the ice-cream. Beat well.
2. Add the sugar, curds and lemon juice. Place on ice and stir for 10 minutes.
3. When thick, pour over the crust. Put to set in the refrigerator.
4. When set, remove and serve with cherry sauce or peach sauce.

   ★ If you like, decorate with cream.

CHERRY SAUCE/PEACH SAUCE

1 small can (450 grams) cherries *or* peaches
2 teaspoons cornflour
2 teaspoons sugar
2 teaspoons lemon juice
a few drops cochineal (for cherry sauce only)

1. Stone the cherries (or chop the peaches). Keep aside the syrup.
2. To the fruit syrup, add the cornflour and sugar.
3. Boil for a little time. Stir till it becomes thick. Then add the lemon juice and fruit (also cochineal in case of cherry sauce). Pour the hot mixture into a bowl and chill.

PEAR PIE

This pie will just melt in your mouth.
Preparation time: 20 minutes • Cooking time: 5 minutes • Serves 6 to 8.

1 small can (450 grams) pears
1 packet (100 grams) pineapple jelly
200 grams (7 oz.) fresh cream
3 tablespoons powdered sugar
2 tablespoons fresh curds
6 tablespoons crushed Marie biscuits
4 tablespoons melted butter

1. Slice the pears.
2. Dissolve the jelly in 2 teacups of boiling water. Cool. Put to set partially in the refrigerator.
3. Beat the cream with the sugar until thick.
4. Mix the partially set jelly, curds and three-quarters of the cream. Taste and add more powdered sugar if required.
5. Mix the biscuits and butter very well and press evenly into a 175 or 200 mm. (7" or 8") diameter loose bottom tin. Place in the refrigerator until the crust is firm.
6. Arrange the pear slices on top of the crust.
7. Pour the jelly mixture over the crust and put to set in the refrigerator.
8. When set, remove the pie from the tin. Decorate with remaining cream and pears.

★ Cut into slices and serve. If you like, sprinkle a little praline powder, *page 119,* on top.

STRAWBERRY SLICE

A simple yet attractive pudding, ideal for tea parties.
Preparation time: 15 minutes ● Cooking time: 5 minutes ● Serves 6 to 8.

For the biscuit crust
6 tablespoons crushed Marie biscuits
4 tablespoons melted butter (approx.)
2 teaspoons sugar

For the filling
1 packet (100 grams) strawberry *or* raspberry jelly
200 grams (7 oz.) fresh cream
3 tablespoons powdered sugar
1 teacup sliced strawberries

For the biscuit crust
1. Mix the biscuits, butter and sugar and press the mixture evenly into a 200 mm. (8") diameter loose bottom flan tin.
2. Place in the refrigerator until firm.

For the filling
1. Dissolve the jelly in 2 teacups of boiling water. Cool. Put to set partially in the refrigerator.
2. Beat the cream with the sugar lightly.
3. Mix the semi-set jelly and three-quarters of the cream very well. If you like, add a little lèmon juice to taste.
4. Spread the sliced strawberries over the chilled crust, keeping aside a few for decoration. Pour the jelly mixture on top and put to set in the refrigerator.

How to serve
1. Remove the pudding from the flan tin, spread the remaining cream and decorate with sliced strawberries.
2. Cut into small pieces and serve.

CREPES BELLE HELENE

Delicious crepes served with peaches and chocolate. An elegant way to end your party.

Preparation time: 5 minutes ● Cooking time: 20 minutes ● Serves 6.

For the pancakes
½ teacup plain flour
½ teacup cornflour
½ teacup milk
½ teacup water
2 teaspoons melted ghee *or* butter

For the pear filling
6 fresh pears *or* 1 small can (450 grams) pears
3 tablespoons sugar (for fresh pears only)
1 teaspoon lemon juice
½ teaspoon grated lemon rind

For the topping
100 grams (4 oz.) fresh cream
1½ tablespoons sugar
25 grams (1 oz.) grated bitter chocolate
2 tablespoons sliced almonds
vanilla ice-cream to serve

For the pancakes
Mix the ingredients and prepare pancakes on a non-stick frying pan using ghee.

For the pear filling
1. Peel, core and slice the pears.
2. Add the sugar, lemon juice, lemon rind and ¾ teacup of water and cook until soft.
3. Chop finely. Keep aside the juice.

How to proceed
1. Beat the cream with the sugar.
2. To the chocolate, add 1 tablespoon of the cream and heat till it melts. Mix with the rest of the cream.
3. Fill each pancake with some pear filling along with a little of its juices.
4. Place the pancakes on a baking dish and spread the sweetened cream on them. Sprinkle the sliced almonds on top and bake in a hot oven at 200°C (400°F) for 5 minutes.

★ Serve warm with vanilla ice-cream.

Variation: PEAR PANCAKES WITH ORANGE SAUCE Prepare the pancakes and pear filling as above but substitute the topping by orange sauce as under.

For the orange sauce
1 teacup orange juice
3 teaspoons sugar
2 level teaspoons cornflour
a few drops orange colouring
a few drops orange essence
½ teaspoon lemon juice

For the orange sauce
1. Mix the orange juice, sugar and cornflour and cook until thick.
2. Add the colouring, essence and lemon juice.

To flambé (optional)
2 to 3 tablespoons brandy

How to proceed
1. Spread the orange sauce over the pancakes and bake in a hot oven at 200°C (400°F) for 5 to 10 minutes.
2. Alternatively, flambé the pancakes by warming the brandy on a low flame, lighting it and pouring over the pancakes.

   ★ Serve hot with or without vanilla ice-cream.

LEMON AND COFFEE DELIGHT

An easy everyday pudding.
Preparation time: 15 minutes ● Cooking time: 5 minutes ● Serves 6 to 8.

1 packet (100 grams) lemon jelly
1 teaspoon instant coffee
200 grams (7 oz.) fresh cream
3 tablespoons powdered sugar
crushed Marie biscuits for
    decoration

1. Dissolve the jelly in 2 teacups of boiling water.
2. Cool. Pour 2 tablespoons of the jelly into a mould and put to set in the refrigerator.
3. Add the coffee to the remaining jelly, pour into a broad vessel and put to set partially in the refrigerator.
4. Beat the cream with the sugar until thick. Mix with the semi-set jelly and pour into the mould tin over the set lemon jelly. Put once again to set in the refrigerator.
5. Just before serving, dip the mould in hot water for a few seconds, loosen the sides and unmould on a plate.

   ★ Sprinkle crushed Marie biscuits on top and serve cold.

PEACH CRUMBLE

A hot pudding for cold days.
Preparation time: 10 minutes ● Cooking time: 30 minutes ● Serves 6 to 8.

1   large can (850 grams) peaches
½ teaspoon cinnamon powder
3   tablespoons raisins
4   tablespoons brown sugar
50 grams (2 oz.) plain flour
25 grams (1 oz.) butter
100 grams (4 oz.) fresh cream

1. Drain the peaches and arrange on a baking dish.
2. Sprinkle the cinnamon powder, raisins and 2 tablespoons of brown sugar over the peaches.
3. Apply the butter to the flour and add 1 tablespoon of brown sugar. Sprinkle over the peaches.
4. Bake in a moderate oven at 180°C (350°F) for ½ hour.
5. Beat the cream and spread over the pudding. Sprinkle the remaining brown sugar on top.

★ Serve immediately or after melting the brown sugar by baking in a hot oven at 200°C (400°F) for 5 minutes.

X. Cakes

CHOCOLATE VELVET CAKE

Velvety smooth in touch and taste.
Preparation time: 20 minutes ● Cooking time: 20 minutes ● Serves 6 to 8.

For the cake
1 three-egg fatless chocolate
   sponge cake mixture, *page 120*
1 teaspoon vanilla essence

To be mixed into a soaking syrup (for the cake)
½ teacup water
3 teaspoons powdered sugar

Other ingredients
200 grams (7 oz.) fresh cream
3 tablespoons powdered sugar
50 grams (2 oz.) grated chocolate
1 teaspoon butter
2 tablespoons chopped walnuts

For the cake
1. Add the essence to the cake mixture. Pour into a well-greased and dusted 200 mm. (8") diameter tin and bake in a hot oven at 200°C (400°F) for 15 minutes. The cake is ready when it leaves the sides of the tin and is springy to touch.
2. Cool the cake and divide into 2 parts horizontally.
3. Sprinkle the soaking syrup on both the cake parts.

How to proceed
1. Beat the cream with the sugar until thick.
2. Spread a little sweetened cream over one cake part and put the other part on top. Spread the remaining cream on the top and sides.
3. Melt the chocolate with the butter and 1 teaspoon of water on a slow flame. Trickle this melted chocolate all over the cake.
4. Sprinkle walnuts on top.

★ Cut into slices and serve cold.

Variation: CHOCOLATE VELVET CAKE (EGGLESS) Proceed as above using eggless chocolate sponge cake mixture, *page 121,* instead of fatless chocolate sponge cake mixture.

RAINBOW CAKE

Children's delight.
Preparation time: 20 minutes ● Cooking time: 20 minutes ● Serves 6 to 8.

For the cakes
2 two-egg fatless sponge cake mixture, *page 120*

For the filling and decoration
1 small can (450 grams) pineapple slices
200 grams (7 oz.) fresh cream
3 tablespoons powdered sugar
½ packet (100 grams for full packet) red jelly
½ packet (100 grams for full packet) yellow *or* orange jelly

For the cakes
1. Pour each cake mixture into a well greased and dusted 175 mm. (7") diameter tin and bake in a hot oven at 200°C (400°F) for 15 minutes. The cake is ready when it leaves the sides of the tin and is springy to touch.
2. Cool the cake.
3. Prepare two cakes in this manner.

How to proceed
1. Dissolve the red jelly in 1½ teacups of boiling water. Cool a little and put to set partially in the refrigerator.
2. Repeat with the yellow jelly.
3. Make small holes in each cake at intervals of about 25 mm. (1").
4. Chop the pineapple slices finely. Keep aside the syrup from the can.
5. Sprinkle a little of the pineapple syrup over both the cake pieces.
6. Place one piece of cake in a cake tin and pour the semi-set red jelly into the holes. Repeat with the other cake using the semi-set yellow jelly. Put both cakes to set in a refrigerator. Separately put the balance semi-set jellies to set in the refrigerator.
7. Beat the cream with the sugar until thick.
8. Dip the cake tins in hot water for a few seconds and remove from the tins.
9. Spread a little sweetened cream on the top of one cake and put the other cake on top.
10. Cut the balance set jellies into pieces.
11. Cover the cake top fully with cream. Sprinkle pineapple pieces and the balance jelly pieces all over. If you like, sprinkle cherry pieces also.

★ Chill the cake and serve after cutting into pieces.

Variation: RAINBOW CAKE (EGGLESS) Proceed as above using eggless sponge cake mixture, *page 121,* instead of fatless sponge cake mixture.

STRAWBERRY LAYERED CAKE

So simple to make, so delicious in taste.
Preparation time: 10 minutes ● No cooking ● Serves 6 to 8.

18 Nice biscuits
200 grams (7 oz.) fresh cream
3 tablespoons powdered sugar
2 teacups sliced strawberries
1 teacup (approx.) orange juice
grated chocolate for decoration

1. Beat the cream with the sugar until thick.
2. Dip 6 biscuits in the orange juice and arrange on a plate. Spread some sweetened cream over these and then place a few strawberries on top.
3. Make two more layers in this way.
4. Finally, cover the cake with the balance cream.
5. Chill.
6. Just before serving, sprinkle grated chocolate on top and decorate with the balance strawberries.

★ Cut into pieces and serve chilled.

Variation: PEACH LAYERED CAKE In the above recipe, increase the quantity of fresh cream and powdered sugar to 300 grams (10½ oz.) and 5 tablespoons respectively; and substitute the strawberries by 1 small can (450 grams) of peaches. Mash three-quarters of the peaches and use these mixed with 2 tablespoons of the sweetened cream (step 1) instead of the sliced strawberries. Use the balance peaches for decoration. If you like, use praline powder, *page 119,* instead of grated chocolate for decoration.

NUTTY CAKE

You will love to munch this cake. Ideal for picnics and outings.
Preparation time: 15 minutes ● Cooking time: 20 minutes ● Serves 6 to 8.

100 grams (4 oz.) butter
8 to 10 Marie biscuits (crumbled)
2 tablespoons cocoa
1 can (400 grams) condensed milk
2 tablespoons chopped walnuts
2 tablespoons chopped
  cashewnuts
1 tablespoon chopped cherries

1. Grease a 200 to 225 mm. (8″ to 9″) diameter cake tin.
2. Mix the biscuit crumbs and butter and press on the bottom of the tin.
3. Sprinkle the cocoa on top.
4. Pour the condensed milk over this.
5. Sprinkle the nuts and cherries uniformly on top.
6. Bake in a moderate hot oven at 190°C (375°F) for 20 minutes.
7. Remove from the oven and keep aside without touching for at least 10 minutes.

 ★ Invert, cut into slices and serve.

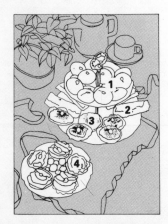

1. CHOCOLATE CHIP COOKIES, *Page 98*
2. FUDGE FINGERS, *Page 98*
3. CHEESY LEMON TARTS, *Page 97*
4. MANGO TARTS, *Page 99*

COCOA FUDGE CAKE (EGGLESS)

An ideal tea-time snack, relished both by adults and children.
Preparation time: 30 minutes ● Cooking time: 40 minutes ● Serves 15.

For the cake
2 teacups plain flour
½ teacup cocoa
½ teaspoon soda bi-carb
1 teaspoon baking powder
1½ teacups powdered sugar
½ teacup fresh curds
½ teacup milk
1 teaspoon vanilla essence
½ teacup melted butter

For the soaking syrup
2 tablespoons sugar
¾ teacup water
3 tablespoons rum (optional)

For the icing
½ teacup sugar
2 tablespoons butter
2 tablespoons cocoa
½ teacup milk
½ teacup icing sugar
½ teaspoon vanilla essence

For decoration
walnuts

For the cake
1. Mix the curds, milk, essence and butter.
2. Beat in the dry ingredients together to form a smooth slack mixture.
3. Pour into two greased and dusted 225 mm. (9") diameter tins and bake in a moderately hot oven at 190°C (375°F) for 25 to 30 minutes. Cool.

For the soaking syrup
1. Boil the sugar and water until it becomes almost half in volume.
2. Cool and add the rum.

For the icing
1. Mix the sugar, butter, cocoa and milk.
2. Bring the mixture to the boil and boil for around 2 minutes while stirring all the time.
3. Remove from the heat.
4. Beat in the icing sugar and vanilla essence till a smooth spreading consistency is obtained.

How to proceed
1. Sprinkle the soaking syrup over both the cakes.
2. Sandwich the cakes with the icing and cover the sides and top with icing.
3. Decorate with walnuts.

★ Cut into slices and serve.

Variation 1: COCOA FUDGE CAKE (WITH EGG) Instead of the above cake, use the fatless chocolate sponge cake, *page 120*.

1. STUFFED MUSHROOMS, *Page 117*
2. VEGETABLE BURGERS, *Page 103*
3. MINI PIZZAS, *Page 104*

ORANGE AND LEMON GATEAU PICTURE ON PAGE 76

A blend of citrus juices enlivens this gateau.
Preparation time: 20 minutes ● Cooking time: 20 minutes ● Serves 6 to 8.

For the cake
1 three-egg fatless sponge cake mixture, *page 120*
4 tablespoons orange juice

For the filling
1 teacup orange juice
6 level teaspoons cornflour
juice of 1 lemon
3 tablespoons sugar
½ teaspoon orange rind
a few drops orange essence
a few drops orange colouring

Other ingredients
200 grams (7 oz.) fresh cream
3 tablespoons powdered sugar
a little grated chocolate *or* praline powder, *page 119*, for decoration

For the cake
1. Pour the cake mixture into a well-greased and dusted 175 mm. (7") diameter tin and bake in a hot oven at 200°C (400°F) for 15 minutes. The cake is ready when it leaves the sides of the tin and is springy to touch.
2. Cool the cake and divide into 2 parts horizontally.
3. Sprinkle the juice over both the cake parts.

For the filling
1. Mix the orange juice, cornflour, lemon juice, sugar and ½ teacup of water. Put to boil and go on stirring and cooking until the mixture becomes thick. Cool.
2. Add the orange rind, essence and colouring.
3. Chill.

How to proceed
1. Beat the cream with the sugar.
2. Add 2 tablespoons of the sweetened cream to the filling.
3. Spread the filling over one cake part and place the other part on top.
4. Cover the entire cake with the balance sweetened cream.
5. Decorate with grated chocolate or praline powder.

★ Cut into slices and serve cold.

Variation: ORANGE AND LEMON GATEAU (EGGLESS) Proceed as above using eggless sponge cake mixture, *page 121*, instead of fatless sponge cake mixture.

XI. Biscuits and Pastries

CHEESY LEMON TARTS PICTURE ON PAGE 93

Lemony and lovely.
Preparation time: 10 minutes ● Cooking time: 15 minutes ● Makes 12 to 15 tarts.

For the shortcrust pastry
100 grams (4 oz.) plain flour
50 grams (2 oz.) soft butter
a pinch salt
ice-cold water to make a dough

For the filling
½ packet (100 grams for full
   packet) lemon jelly
200 grams (7 oz.) fresh cream
3 tablespoons powdered sugar
2 tablespoons fresh curds
½ teaspoon lemon juice
a little grated lemon rind (optional)

For decoration
fruit pieces
grated chocolate

For the shortcrust pastry
1. Sieve the flour with the salt.
2. Rub in the butter and make a dough by adding ice-cold water (about 1 tablespoon).
3. Roll out the dough to about 3 mm. (⅛") thickness.
4. Cut with a fluted cutter of desired size.
5. Press into tart cases and prick with a fork.
6. Bake blind in a hot oven at 230°C (450°F) for 10 to 12 minutes.
7. Cool the tart cases.

For the filling
1. Dissolve the jelly in 1 teacup of boiling water. Cool. Put to set in the refrigerator.
2. When partially set, take out.
3. Beat the cream with the sugar.
4. Add half the cream to the partially set jelly. Add the curds, lemon juice, rind and mix well. Put the mixture into tart moulds and put to set in the refrigerator.

How to serve
1. When set, beat the remaining cream with thick and pipe a little on each tart.
2. Decorate with fruit pieces and grated chocolate.

FUDGE FINGERS PICTURE ON PAGE 93

Adults will love these fingers which are very easy to prepare.
Preparation time: 10 minutes • Cooking time: 5 minutes • Makes 20 pieces.

For the fudge
200 grams (7 oz.) powdered sweet biscuits
100 grams (3½ oz.) butter
100 grams (3½ oz.) sugar
2 tablespoons milk
2 level tablespoons cocoa
½ teaspoon vanilla essence
4 tablespoons chopped walnuts
a pinch salt

For the chocolate icing
1½ teacups icing sugar
3 teaspoons cocoa
2 tablespoons (approx.) hot water

For decoration
desiccated coconut

For the fudge
1. Mix the butter, sugar, milk, cocoa and salt. Heat on a slow flame until it becomes a liquid. Remove from the heat.
2. Add the vanilla essence and walnuts and mix.
3. Pour this mixture over the biscuits. Mix thoroughly.
4. Press the mixture evenly on a Swiss roll tray. Put to set in the refrigerator. This will require about 30 minutes.

For the chocolate icing
Mix the sugar, cocoa and hot water. If you like, add a little extra water.

How to proceed
1. Spread the icing evenly over the fudge.
2. Sprinkle the coconut on top and once again put to set in the refrigerator for about 30 minutes.

★ Cut into pieces and serve.

CHOCOLATE CHIP COOKIES PICTURE ON PAGE 93

Chocolate chips make all the difference.
Preparation time: 20 minutes • Cooking time: 20 minutes • Makes 20 pieces.

170 grams (6 oz.) plain flour
115 grams (4 oz.) butter
55 grams (2 oz.) sugar
1 teaspoon vanilla essence
2 tablespoons roughly chopped chocolate pieces

1. Beat the butter and sugar very well until light and creamy.
2. Add the vanilla essence and beat again.
3. Sieve the flour very well and add to the mixture. Add the chocolate pieces.
4. Shape into small rounds, place on a greased baking tray and bake in a moderately hot oven at 180°C (350°F) for 15 to 20 minutes.

MANGO TARTS PICTURE ON PAGE 93

An instant hit at tea parties. These delicious rich tarts will just melt in your mouth.
Preparation time: 20 minutes ● Cooking time: 20 minutes ● Makes 12 to 15 tarts.

For the tart cases
100 grams (4 oz.) plain flour
50 grams (2 oz.) soft butter
a pinch salt
ice-cold water to make a dough

For the tart cases
1. Sieve the flour with the salt.
2. Rub in the butter and make a dough by adding ice-cold water (about 1 tablespoon).
3. Roll out the dough to about 3 mm. (⅛") thickness.
4. Cut with a fluted cutter of desired size.
5. Press into tart cases and prick with a fork.
6. Bake blind in a hot oven at 230°C (450°F) for 10 to 12 minutes.
7. Cool the tart cases.

For the lemon filling
6 teaspoons lemon juice
3 teaspoons cornflour
2 tablespoons granulated sugar
¾ teacup water
100 grams (4 oz.) fresh cream
1 tablespoon powdered sugar
¼ teaspoon grated lemon rind
a little yellow colouring (optional)

For the lemon filling
1. Mix the lemon juice, cornflour, granulated sugar and add ¾ teacup of water.
2. Cook on a slow flame until the mixture becomes thick.
3. Cool.
4. Beat the cream with the powdered sugar and add to the mixture.
5. Add the lemon rind and yellow colouring.
6. Chill thoroughly.

Other ingredients
2 tablespoons mixed fruit jam
2 mangoes, cut into slices

How to proceed
1. Fill each tart with about ¼ teaspoon of jam.
2. Put a large blob of lemon filling on top.
3. Cover with mango slices of the appropriate length.
4. Warm the remaining jam and brush on top of the mango slices.
5. Store in the refrigerator.

★ Serve cold.

PEAR PASTRIES

An attractive pastry which tastes as good as it looks.
Preparation time: 20 minutes ● Cooking time: 20 minutes ● Makes 15 pastries.

1 three-egg fatless sponge cake
   mixture (*page 120*)
1 small can (400 grams) pears
100 grams (4 oz.) fresh cream
1 tablespoon powdered sugar

For the lemon filling
5 teaspoons lemon juice
2 tablespoons sugar
2 tablespoons cornflour
¾ teacup water
¼ teaspoon grated lemon rind

Other ingredients
2 tablespoons melted jam
2 tablespoons crushed biscuits

1. Pour the cake mixture into a well-greased and dusted Swiss roll tin and bake in a hot oven at 200°C (400°F) for 15 minutes. The cake is ready when it leaves the sides of the tin and is springy to touch.
2. Cool the cake and cut into rounds (or squares).
3. Sprinkle a little syrup from the pear can over the cake pieces.
4. Slice the pears.
5. Mix all the ingredients for the lemon filling except for the lemon rind and boil until the mixture becomes thick. Cool.
6. Beat the cream with the sugar until thick.
7. Add the lemon mixture and lemon rind and mix well.

How to proceed
1. Spread a little lemon filling on each cake round and put another cake round on top.
2. Apply a little lemon filling on the upper cake round top and thereafter arrange a few pear slices on top. Apply a little jam on the sides. Apply crushed biscuits over the jam.
3. Repeat with the remaining cake and filling.
4. Chill the pastries.
5. Place in paper cups and serve.

Variation: PEAR PASTRIES (EGGLESS) Proceed as above using eggless sponge cake mixture, *page 121,* instead of fatless sponge mixture.

TWO IN ONE COOKIES

Crunchy and delicious.
Preparation time: 20 minutes ● Cooking time: 25 minutes ● Makes 15 to 20 pieces.

For the cookie mixture
170 grams (6 oz.) plain flour
115 grams (4 oz.) white butter
55 grams (2 oz.) powdered sugar
1 teaspoon vanilla essence

For the cashewnut mixture
50 grams (2 oz.) butter
50 grams (2 oz.) powdered sugar
¼ teaspoon almond essence
75 grams (3 oz.) powdered
   cashewnuts

For the cookie mixture
1. Beat the butter and sugar very well until light and creamy.
2. Add the vanilla essence and beat again.
3. Sieve the flour very well and add to the mixture. Mix well.
4. Roll out the dough to about 6 mm. (¼″) thickness. Stamp out rounds with a cutter.
5. Place the rolled cookies in a greased muffin tray.

For the cashewnut mixture
1. Beat the butter and sugar.
2. Add the almond essence and beat again.
3. Add the cashewnuts.

How to proceed
1. Put about ½ teaspoon of the cashewnut mixture on each cookie.
2. Bake in a moderate oven at 180°C (350°F) for 25 minutes.

ALMOND ROCKS PICTURE ON PAGE 75

Send these mouth-watering rocks as gifts on special occasions.
Preparation time: 10 minutes • Cooking time: 25 minutes • Makes 50 pieces.

400 grams (14 oz.) small almonds
400 grams (14 oz.) plain chocolate
100 grams (3½ oz.) milk chocolate

1. Roast the almonds in an oven for 10 to 15 minutes.
2. Grate the chocolates, place in a tray and heat in a moderate oven at 180°C (350°F) for about 10 minutes.
3. Remove from the oven and continually stir the chocolate until it cools a little. Add the almonds and mix well.
4. Put small pieces of coated almonds on a tray lined with grease proof paper or aluminium foil. Keep in the refrigerator for 2 hours.
5. Wrap in decorative foil and store in the refrigerator.

Note: If using large almonds, break into small pieces before baking.

Variation: CASHEW ROCKS Instead of small almonds, use the same quantity of cashewnuts broken into small pieces.

XII. Snacks

VEGETABLE BURGERS PICTURE ON PAGE 94

A wholesome filling snack — everybody's favourite.
Preparation time: 25 minutes ● Cooking time: 20 minutes ● Makes 10 to 12 burgers.

For the vegetable cutlets
4   teacups mixed boiled vegetables
3   boiled and mashed potatoes
2   slices bread
2   teaspoons chilli-ginger paste
2   teaspoons lemon juice
1   teaspoon garam masala
salt to taste
bread crumbs
oil

For the salad
3   teacups shredded cabbage
2   grated carrots
200 grams (7 oz.) fresh cream
3   teaspoons sugar
1   teaspoon mustard powder
1½ teaspoons salt
3   tablespoons salad oil

For the burgers
10 to 12 buns

For the filling
cucumber slices
tomato slices
lettuce leaves
tomato ketchup
mustard sauce

For the vegetable cutlets
1. Dip the bread slices in water for a few seconds. Squeeze out the water.
2. Mix the vegetables, potatoes, bread, paste, lemon juice, garam masala and salt and shape into small flattened rounds.
3. Sprinkle bread crumbs all over.
4. Cook on a tawa (griddle) with oil.

For the salad
1. Beat the cream with the sugar.
2. Add the remaining ingredients and mix thoroughly. Chill.

How to serve
1. Cut each bun horizontally into two.
2. Spread a little tomato ketchup and mustard sauce on the lower half.
3. Place a lettuce leaf and vegetable cutlet on top.
4. Spread a little salad and put a few cucumber slices and one tomato slice on top.
5. Cover with the upper half of the bun.
6. Heat below the grill for a few minutes.
7. Repeat with the remaining buns, cutlets, salad and filling.

★ Serve hot in folded napkins.

103

MINI PIZZAS PICTURE ON PAGE 94

So mini, so delicious. A delightful tea-time snack.
Preparation time: 1 hour • Cooking time: 20 minutes • Serves 6.

For the pizza dough
250 grams (9 oz.) plain flour
10 grams (⅓ oz.) fresh yeast *or*
   1 teaspoon dry yeast
2 teaspoons oil
½ teaspoon sugar
½ teaspoon salt

For the pizza dough
1. Sieve the flour with the sugar and salt.
2. Add the oil and mix well.
3. Make a well in the centre. Crumble the yeast and put in this well.
4. Sprinkle ½ teacup of warm water over the yeast. Wait for 5 minutes.
5. Mix the yeast with the flour. Add enough water to make a semi-soft dough.
6. Knead the dough for 5 to 7 minutes.
7. Cover the dough with a wet cloth and leave for 45 minutes or until double in size.
8. Knead the dough for 1 minute.

For the filling
1 packet (200 grams) fresh mushrooms *or* 2 teacups cooked corn
1 chopped onion
1 chopped capsicum
1 tablespoon oil
1 teaspoon lemon juice
2 chopped green chillies
salt to taste

For the filling
1. Heat the oil and fry the onion for 1 minute.
2. Add the capsicums and green chillies and fry again for 1 minute.
3. Chop the mushrooms.
4. Add the chopped mushrooms, lemon juice and salt and cook for 3 minutes.
5. Drain.

For the pizza sauce
500 grams (1⅛ lb.) red tomatoes
1 onion, chopped
3 cloves garlic, crushed
½ teaspoon chilli powder
1 teaspoon sugar (approx.)
2 tablespoons oil
salt to taste

For the pizza sauce
1. Chop the tomatoes. Drain the liquid.
2. Heat the oil and fry the onion and garlic for 1 to 2 minutes.
3. Add the chopped tomatoes, chilli powder, sugar and salt and boil until the tomatoes are soft.
4. Blend in a liquidiser.

For the baking

1 teacup white sauce, *page 123*
5 to 6 tablespoons grated cheese

How to proceed

1. Roll out the dough into thin puris to fit a muffin tray.
2. Grease a muffin tray thoroughly and press the puris inside.
3. After 10 minutes, spread a little filling, plenty of pizza sauce and a little white sauce on each round.
4. Sprinkle the cheese on top and bake in a hot oven at 200°C (400°F) for 10 to 12 minutes.

★ Serve hot.

Note: Instead of the above pizza dough, you can straightaway use readymade pizza bread.

POTATO BAKE

You will find this simple dish surprisingly tasty.
Preparation time: 10 minutes ● Cooking time: 1¼ hours ● Serves 4 to 6.

1 kg. (2¼ lb.) potatoes
50 grams (2 oz.) butter
175 grams (6 oz.) grated cheese
300 ml. (10 fl. oz.) milk *or* light cream
salt and freshly ground black pepper to taste

1. Wash the potatoes and slice them thinly in a round shape.
2. In a greased baking dish, make alternate layers of some potatoes and of cheese with knobs of butter ending with a layer of cheese and butter.
3. Season the milk with salt and freshly powdered black pepper and pour over the potato layer.
4. Cover and bake in a medium oven at 180°C (350°F). After 45 minutes to 1 hour, remove the cover and continue baking until the potatoes are tender and the top is browned.

★ Serve hot.

CHEESY TARTS

An excellent snack for cocktails, tea parties etc.
Preparation time: 30 minutes ● Cooking time: 30 minutes ● Makes
40 small tarts..

For the tart cases
100 grams (4 oz.) plain flour
50 grams (2 oz.) soft butter
a pinch salt
ice cold water to make a dough

For the cheese filling
5 to 7 tablespoons cooking
     cheese
1 tablespoon chooped onion
½ teaspoon chopped green chilli
1 tablespoon plain flour
1 teacup milk
1 teaspoon mustard powder
     mixed with a little water
2 tablespoons butter

For the tart cases
1. Sieve the flour with the salt.
2. Rub in the butter and make a dough by
   adding 1 tablespoon of ice-cold water.
   Knead well.
3. Roll out the dough to about 3 mm. (⅛")
   thickness.
4. Cut with a fluted cutter of desired size.
5. Press into tart cases and prick with a fork.
6. Bake blind in a hot oven at 230°C (450°F)
   for 10 to 12 minutes.
7. Cool the tart cases.

For the cheese filling
1. Heat the butter and fry the onion on a
   slow flame for 2 minute.
2. Add the green chilli and flour and fry
   again for ½ minute.
3. Add the milk. Go on stirring and cooking
   the mixture until it becomes thick.
4. Add the mustard and 5 tablespoons
   of the cheese and mix.

How to proceed
1. Fill each tart case with a little cheesy
   mixture. If you like, sprinkle the balance
   cheese on top.
2. Grill for 3 to 4 minutes.

   ★ Serve hot.

CHOLA METHI DHOKLA

You will love these entirely novel dhoklas.
Preparation time: 20 minutes ● Cooking time: 15 to 20 minutes ● Serves 6 to 8.

1 teacup chola dal (dal of black eyed beans) *or* moong dal
2 teacups fresh fenugreek leaves (methi bhaji)
5 green chillies
¼ teaspoon asafoetida
2 tablespoons fresh curds
1 teaspoon baking powder
2 teaspoons oil
2 pinches soda bi-carb
salt to taste

1. Soak the dal for 4 hours.
2. Grind the soaked dal with the green chillies adding a little water.
3. Add the asafoetida and salt.
4. Mix the curds and baking powder and add.
5. Add the oil and keep the batter aside for 2 to 3 hours.
6. Sprinkle the soda bi-carb and salt over the fenugreek leaves.
7. Grease small ring mould tins (the number corresponding to the volume of the batter). Put a few fenugreek leaves in each ring and fill with a little batter. Steam for 5 to 7 minutes.

★ Serve hot with green chutney.

MOONG DAL TOAST

A delicious and unusual combination.
Preparation time: 20 minutes ● Cooking time: 20 minutes ● Makes 20 pieces.

10 to 12 bread slices
1 teacup moong dal
4 green chillies
½ teacup chopped cabbage
1 chopped onion
a pinch asafoetida
1 tablespoon gram flour (optional)
½ teaspoon soda bi-carb
½ teaspoon lemon juice
1 tablespoon chopped coriander
salt to taste
butter *or* ghee for cooking
chutney *or* tomato ketchup to serve

1. Soak the moong dal overnight.
2. Next day, grind the soaked dal and the green chillies in a liquidiser.
3. Add the cabbage, onion, asafoetida, gram flour, soda bi-carb, lemon juice, coriander and salt. Keep aside for 1 hour.
4. Spread a little moong dal mixture on each bread slice.
5. Cook in a non-stick frying pan with the help of a little butter.

★ Cut into small pieces and serve hot with chutney or tomato ketchup.

CORN AND SPINACH CREAM CRACKER SNACK

Always a hit at cocktail parties.
Preparation time: 20 minutes ● Cooking time: 10 minutes ● Makes 36 pieces.

For the corn filling
1 can (450 grams) cream-style
   sweet corn
2 chopped onions
1 tablespoon chopped coriander
3 chopped green chillies
juice of 1 lemon
3 tablespoons oil
salt to taste

For the spinach filling
4 teacups chopped spinach
1 chopped onion
2 chopped green chillies
a pinch soda-bi-carb
2 teacups milk
1 tablespoon plain flour
1 tablespoon butter
salt to taste

Other ingredients
3 dozen cream cracker biscuits
4 tablespoons cooking cheese
Tabasco sauce

For the corn filling
1. Heat the oil, add the onions and cook for 1 minute.
2. Add the corn, coriander, chillies, lemon juice and salt and cook for 2 minutes.

For the spinach filling
1. Heat the butter and fry the onion for ½ minute. Add the green chillies and fry again for a few seconds.
2. Add the spinach and soda-bi-carb and cook for 2 minutes. Drain.
3. Mix the milk with the flour, add to the mixture and cook until the mixture becomes thick. Add salt.

How to proceed
1. Spread a little corn filling and some spinach mixture on each cream cracker. Top with a little cheese and dot with Tabasco sauce.
2. Grill in a hot oven at 200°C(400°F) for a few minutes.

   ★ Serve hot.

GRILLED VEGETABLE TOAST

Simple to make — delicious to eat.
Preparation time: 10 minutes ● Cooking time: 5 to 10 minutes ● Makes 24 toasts.

6 to 8 bread slices
2 tablespoons soft butter
2 teaspoons milk
6 tablespoons grated cheese
1 chopped onion
1 chopped tomato
2 tablespoons cooked corn (optional)
1 teaspoon mustard powder
2 chopped green chillies
salt to taste
Tabasco sauce to serve

1. Mix the butter, milk and cheese.
2. Add the onion, tomato, corn, mustard powder, green chillies and salt.
3. Toast the bread slices.
4. On one side of each bread slice, spread a little vegetable mixture.
5. Place the bread slices below the grill for a few minutes.
6. When toasted, cut into pieces and serve hot with Tabasco sauce.

MUSHROOM SNACK

A sophisticated cocktail snack.
Preparation time: 10 minutes ● Cooking time: 10 minutes ● Serves 10 to 12.

400 grams (14 oz.) canned mushrooms
500 grams (1⅛ lb.) salted biscuits *or* crackers
1 chopped onion
2 cloves crushed garlic
2 tablespoons plain flour
1 chopped green chilli (optional)
4 tablespoons grated cheese
1 teacup milk
2 tablespoons butter

1. Chop the mushrooms. Keep aside the liquid from the can.
2. Heat the butter and fry the onion and garlic for 1 minute.
3. Add the flour and fry again for a little while.
4. Add the mushrooms, half of the cheese, the milk, green chilli and 1 teacup of the mushroom liquid and cook for a few minutes.
5. Spread the mixture on crackers and arrange on a greased baking tray.
6. Sprinkle the balance cheese on top and bake in a hot oven at 200°C (400°F) for 10 to 12 minutes.

★ Serve hot.

Variation: Instead of mushrooms, use an equivalent quantity of canned sweet corn or of mixed boiled vegetables.

CORN SPINACH AND RICE BALLS PICTURE ON FACING PAGE

Corn, spinach and rice make a tasty, wholesome snack.
Preparation time: 10 minutes • Cooking time: 20 minutes • Serves 12.

2   teacups cooked rice
1   teacup cooked corn
3   tablespoons finely chopped and
    boiled spinach
2   tablespoons chopped coriander
3   chopped green chillies
2   tablespoons grated cheese
salt to taste
oil for deep frying

For the sauce
1½ teacups milk
5   level tablespoons plain flour
4   tablespoons butter

For the batter
½ teacup plain flour
1   teacup water
bread crumbs

To serve
tomato ketchup

For the sauce
1. Melt the butter, add the flour and cook for
   1 minute.
2. Add the milk and go on cooking and
   stirring till the sauce is thick. Remove
   from the fire.

How to proceed
1. Add the rice, corn, spinach, coriander,
   green chillies, cheese and salt and mix
   well. Shape into round balls.
2. Mix the plain flour and water. Dip the
   balls in the batter, roll into bread crumbs
   and deep fry in oil.

★ Serve hot with tomato ketchup.

1. LETTUCE CUPS, *Page 113*
2. COCO-ORANGE DRINK, *Page 15*
3. GREEN GODDESS, *Page 15*
4. CREAMY MUSHROOMS, *Page 115*
5. CORN SPINACH AND RICE BALLS, *Above*

LETTUCE CUPS PICTURE ON PAGE 111

You can serve these cups as a salad or as an accompaniment to drinks.
Preparation time: 15 minutes ● No cooking ● Serves 15.

a few lettuce leaves
2 teacups, chopped fruits (apples, pears, bananas, stone cherries)
1 teacup grated carrots
2 tablespoons roasted peanuts, broken into pieces (optional)

For the curds dressing
1 teacup thick curds
2 tablespoons fresh cream
1 grated cucumber
½ teaspoon chopped green chillies
salt to taste

For the curds dressing
1. Tie the curds in a muslin cloth and hang up for about 2 hours.
2. Squeeze a little water from the cucumber and then mix the curds and cream.
3. Add the green chillies and salt. Chill thoroughly.

How to serve
1. Put the lettuce leaves and carrots in separate bowls of cold water for about 30 minutes. Drain thereafter.
2. Tear the lettuce leaves into small pieces, approximately square in size. Make smaller pieces if serving as an accompaniment.
3. Arrange the lettuce pieces in one corner of a large tray, fruits in another and carrots in the third leaving sufficient margin in the centre.
4. Put the dressing in a bowl and sprinkle nuts on top. Place the bowl in the centre of the tray.
5. Let the guests help themselves by putting some fruit on lettuce leaves, a little dressing on top and finally sprinkling carrots on it.

VEGETABLE FRANKIE

A mouthwatering snack. Once you have tasted it, you will always ask for more.
Preparation time: 30 minutes ● Cooking time: 20 minutes ● Serves 6 to 8.

For the puris
250 grams (9 oz.) plain flour
2 slices white bread
½ teaspoon salt
1 tablespoon ghee (optional)
ghee for deep frying

For the potato rolls
6 to 7 boiled and mashed
   potatoes
¾ teacup boiled and mashed
   green peas
½ teacup grated cheese
3 chopped green chillies
1 teaspoon garam masala
1 teaspoon lemon juice
salt to taste
½ teacup plain flour mixed with
   1 teacup water and pinch salt
bread crumbs
oil for deep frying

To be mixed into masala water
2 teaspoons amchur powder
1 teaspoon chilli powder
½ teaspoon garam masala
¼ teaspoon salt
¾ teacup water

**To be mixed into onion masala
mixture**
2 chopped onions
1 teaspoon chilli powder
1 teaspoon amchur powder
½ teaspoon salt

To serve
green chillies in vinegar

For the puris
1. Sieve the flour.
2. Soak the bread slices in water for a few minutes. Squeeze out the water and crumble thoroughly.
3. Add the crumbled bread, salt and ghee (if you like frankies softer) to the flour and make a dough by adding water.
4. Roll out into thick puris and deep fry very lightly in ghee. Alternatively, roll out into thin puris and cook each puri on a tawa (griddle) on both sides for a few seconds.

For the potato rolls
1. Mix the potatoes, green peas, grated cheese, chillies, garam masala, lemon juice and salt and shape into long rolls of the size of the puris.
2. Make a batter by mixing the flour, water and salt.
3. Dip the rolls in this batter, roll into bread crumbs and deep fry in oil.

How to proceed
1. On a small tawa, cook each puri on both sides for a few minutes. If you like, use a little ghee and fry lightly.
2. On each puri, apply a little masala water, sprinkle a little onion masala mixture and chillies in vinegar.

★ Put a potato roll in the centre, fold and serve immediately.

XIII. Cooking in a hurry

CREAMY MUSHROOMS PICTURE ON PAGE 111

For the mushroom lovers. Can be served as a cocktail snack or as a main dish (serves 2).
Preparation time: a few minutes ● Cooking time: a few minutes ● Serves 10 to 15.

1 can (400 grams) mushrooms
1 tablespoon chopped onion
4 tablespoons fresh cream
½ teaspoon mixed herbs *or*
   1 tablespoon chopped parsley
1 teaspoon butter
a pinch salt
a pinch pepper

1. Drain the mushrooms.
2. Heat the butter and fry the onion for ½ minute.
3. Add the mushrooms and fry for a further 1 minute.
4. Add the cream, herbs, salt and pepper and mix well.

   ★ Serve hot with toothpicks.

SIMPLE CAESAR SALAD PICTURE ON PAGE 112

A simple adaptation of the world famous salad.
Preparation time: a few minutes ● Cooking time: 10 minutes ● Serves 6.

2 heads lettuce
3 to 4 tablespoons cheese cubes
2 to 3 spring onions
1 teacup fried bread croutons

For the dressing
2 tablespoons salad oil
1 tablespoon vinegar
½ teaspoon sugar
½ teaspoon salt
¼ teaspoon pepper

1. Chop the lettuce. Chop the spring onions. Place in cold water for 10 minutes.
2. Remove from the cold water and place in a serving bowl. Add the cheese cubes and croutons.
3. Shake the dressing ingredients in a bottle and pour over the salad.

   ★ Toss and serve.

FRUIT AND JELLY PIE PICTURE ON PAGE 112

Colourful and tempting, yet easy to prepare.
Preparation time: 10 minutes ● Cooking time: 10 minutes ● Serves 6 to 8.

For the crust
6 tablespoons crushed Marie biscuits
4 tablespoons melted butter
1 tablespoon sugar

For the filling
1 packet (100 grams) orange *or* raspberry jelly
1 can (450 grams) fruit cocktail *or* 1 cup chopped fresh fruit

For decoration
100 grams (4 oz.) fresh cream
2 tablespoons powdered sugar

For the crust
1. Mix the biscuits, butter and sugar very well and press evenly into a 200 or 225 mm. (8" or 9") diameter loose bottom flan tin.
2. Place in the refrigerator until firm.

For the filling
1. Dissolve the jelly in 3 teacups of boiling water. Place over ice and stir continuously.
2. When the jelly gets thicker, add the chopped fruit while stirring continuously.

How to proceed
1. Pour the jelly mixture over the biscuit crust and put to set in the refrigerator.
2. Just before serving, beat the cream with the sugar.

★ Cut into slices and serve with the sweetened cream.

MACARONI IN A HURRY PICTURE ON PAGE 112

A very tasty way of serving this popular pasta.
Preparation time: 10 minutes ● Cooking time: 10 minutes ● Serves 4.

3 teacups boiled macaroni
1 chopped onion
1 chopped capsicum
2 chopped tomatoes
½ teaspoon finely chopped green chilli (optional)
3 tablespoons grated cheese
2 tablespoons butter
1 chopped spring onion
salt to taste

1. Heat the butter and fry the onion for 1 minute.
2. Add the capsicum, tomatoes, green chillies and fry again for 1 minute.
3. Add the macaroni, cheese and salt and sprinkle the spring onion on top.

★ Serve hot.

SPINACH SOUP PICTURE ON PAGE 18

A nourishing soup, suitable for every occasion.
Preparation time: 5 minutes ● Cooking time: 5 minutes ● Serves 6.

1 teacup chopped spinach
1 chopped onion
3 teacups milk
3 teaspoons cornflour
1 tablespoon butter
salt and pepper to taste
bread croutons for serving

1. Heat the butter and fry the onions for 1 minute.
2. Add the spinach and fry again for 1 minute.
3. Mix the milk, cornflour and 3 teacups of water and add to the spinach. Boil for a few minutes.
4. Add salt and pepper.

★ Serve hot with croutons.

STUFFED MUSHROOMS PICTURE ON PAGE 94

A sophisticated snack with the delicate flavour of parsley.
Preparation time: 5 minutes ● Cooking time: 5 minutes ● Makes 20 pieces.

20 fresh large mushrooms
1 teaspoon butter

For the stuffing
1 teacup finely chopped parsley
2 slices fresh bread
1 chopped onion
1 chopped green chilli
a few drops lemon juice
salt to taste

Detach and discard the stems from the mushrooms. Wash the mushroom caps.

For the stuffing
1. Heat the butter and fry the onion on a slow flame for 1 minute.
2. Add the green chillies and fry again for a few seconds.
3. Crumble the bread slices.
4. Add the crumbled bread, parsley, lemon juice and salt and cook for 1 minute.

How to proceed
1. Stuff the cavities of the mushroom caps with the stuffing.
2. Put the butter in a large frying pan and arrange the stuffed mushrooms in it. Cover and cook for 3 to 4 minutes.

★ Serve hot.

GARLIC BREAD

Your friends will love this bread.
Preparation time: a few minutes • Cooking time: 5 minutes • Makes 12 pieces.

6 hot dog rolls
4 to 5 cloves garlic
1 tablespoon butter

1. Divide each hot dog roll in half horizontally.
2. Crush the cloves of garlic and mix with the butter.
3. Apply this butter on the open side of the rolls.
4. Grill in a hot oven at 200°C (400°F) until crisp.

★ Serve hot wrapped in a napkin.

ORANGE DRINK

A creamy and tasty drink.
Preparation time: a few minutes • No cooking • Makes 1 tall glass.

1 tablespoon orange squash
1 teaspoon lemon juice
1 teaspoon fresh cream *or*
  2 teaspoons vanilla ice-cream
½ bottle (200 ml. for full bottle)
  lemonade *or* any lemon drink
crushed ice
pineapple pieces for decoration

1. Mix all the ingredients except pineapple in a shaker and pour into a tall glass.
2. Decorate with pineapple pieces and serve immediately.

QUICK ORANGE MOUSSE

Prepare this pudding whenever unexpected guests turn up.
Preparation time: 10 minutes • Cooking time: 5 minutes • Serves 6 to 8.

1 packet (100 grams) orange jelly
1 family pack (½ litre) vanilla ice-cream
1 teaspoon lemon juice
a few drops orange essence *or* orange colouring
sweetened cream for decoration

1. Dissolve the jelly in 3 teacups of boiling water.
2. Pour over the ice-cream and place over the ice. Add the lemon juice and beat continuously until light and fluffy. Add the orange essence.
3. Pour into individual tall glasses and put to set in the refrigerator.
4. Just before serving, decorate with sweetened cream.

★ Serve cold.

XIV. Basic Recipes

CHOCOLATE SAUCE

Preparation time: 10 minutes ● Cooking time: 10 minutes ● Makes about
3 teacups.

100 grams (4 oz.) plain *or* milk
   chocolate, broken into small
   pieces
1 tablespoon plain flour
½ teacup milk
3 teaspoons cocoa (approx.)
200 grams (7 oz.) beaten cream
4 to 5 tablespoons sugar
½ teaspoon vanilla essence
1 tablespoon butter

1. Melt the butter and fry the flour on a slow
   flame for ½ minute.
2. Add the milk, chocolate pieces, cocoa,
   cream, sugar and 1 teacup of water. Go
   on stirring and cooking on a slow flame
   until the mixture becomes thick.
3. Stir in the essence.

PRALINE POWDER

Preparation time: 10 minutes ● Cooking time: 10 minutes ● Makes about
1 teacup.

¾ teacup almonds *or* cashewnuts
   or peanuts
¾ to 1 teacup sugar

1. Melt the sugar in a heavy saucepan and
   add the nuts.
2. Spread the mixture on a tin and allow to
   cool.
3. Powder coarsely and store in an air-tight
   jar.

GUJARATI KADHI

Preparation time: a few minutes ● Cooking time: 15 minutes ● Serves 4.

2 tablespoons gram flour
2 teacups fresh curds
1 teaspoon chilli-ginger paste
2 curry leaves
2 teaspoons sugar (approx.)
2 tablespoons chopped coriander
salt to taste

For the tempering
½ teaspoon cumin seeds
½ teaspoon mustard seeds
a pinch asafoetida
1 red chilli broken into pieces
2 teaspoons ghee

1. Mix the gram flour, curds and 3 teacups of water. Beat.
2. Add the chilli-ginger paste, curry leaves, sugar and salt and put to boil.
3. Boil whilst stirring for a while.
4. Prepare the tempering by heating the ghee and frying the cumin and mustard seeds until they turn brown. Add the asafoetida and red chilli.
5. Add the tempering to the kadhi and boil for a few minutes.

★ Sprinkle coriander on top and serve hot.

FATLESS SPONGE CAKE

Preparation time: 15 minutes ● Cooking time: 15 minutes.

For large cake
3 large eggs
80 grams (3 oz.) plain flour
80 to 110 grams (3 to 4 oz.) fine tea
   sugar *or* powdered sugar

For small cake
2 large eggs
50 grams (2 oz.) plain flour
50 to 80 grams (2 to 3 oz.) fine tea
   sugar *or* powdered sugar

1. Sieve the flour.
2. Grease and dust a baking tin. Use approx. 250mm. × 125mm. (10" × 5") or 175mm. (7") diameter tin for the large cake, and 225mm. × 100mm. (9" × 4") or 150mm. (6") diameter tin for the small cake.
3. Beat the eggs and sugar very well until thick and double in quantity.
4. Fold in the well-sieved flour carefully and mix gently with a metal spoon.
5. Pour the mixture into the prepared baking tin.
6. Bake in a hot oven at 200°C (400°F) for 15 minutes.
7. The cake is ready when it leaves the sides of the tin and is springy to touch.
8. Take out from the oven and leave for 1 minute. Loosen the sides with a knife, invert the tin over a rack and tap sharply to remove.
9. Cool the cake.

Variation: FATLESS CHOCOLATE SPONGE CAKE Proceed as above adding 1 level teaspoon of cocoa to the flour at step 1.

120

EGGLESS SPONGE CAKE

Preparation time: 10 minutes • Cooking time: 20 minutes.

½ can (400 grams for full can)
  condensed milk
140 grams (5 oz.) self-raising flour
1 level teaspoon baking powder
½ teaspoon soda bi-carb
60 ml. (2 fl.oz.) melted butter *or*
  margarine
1 teaspoon vanilla essence

1. Sieve the flour, baking powder and soda bi-carb together.
2. Mix the flour mixture, condensed milk, melted butter, essence and 75ml. (2½ fl.oz.) water and beat well.
3. Pour the mixture into a greased and dusted 150mm. (6") diameter tin.
4. Bake in a hot oven at 200°C (400°F) for 10 minutes. Then reduce the temperature to 150°C (300°F) and bake for a further 10 minutes.
5. The cake is ready when it leaves the sides of the tin and is springy to touch. When ready, take out from the oven and leave for 1 minute. Invert the tin over a rack and tap sharply to remove.
6. Cool the cake.

EGGLESS CHOCOLATE SPONGE CAKE

Preparation time: 10 minutes • Cooking time: 25 minutes.

½ can (400 grams for full can)
  condensed milk
125 grams (4½ oz.) self-raising
  flour
1 tablespoon cocoa
1 tablespoon chocolate powder
½ teaspoon soda bi-carb
1 level teaspoon baking powder
60 ml. (2 fl.oz.) melted butter *or*
  margarine
1 teaspoon vanilla essence

1. Sieve the flour, cocoa, chocolate powder, baking powder and soda bi-carb together.
2. Mix the condensed milk, flour mixture, 75ml. (2½ fl.oz.) water, the vanilla essence and melted butter thoroughly.
3. Pour the cake mixture into a greased and dusted 150mm. or 175mm. (6" or 7") diameter tin.
4. Bake in a hot oven at 200°C (400°F) for 10 minutes. Then reduce the temperature to 180°C (350°F) and bake for a further 10 minutes.
5. The cake is ready when it leaves the sides of the tin and is springy to touch. When ready, take out from the oven and leave for 1 minute. Invert the tin over a rack and tap sharply to remove.
6. Cool the cake.

APRICOT SAUCE

Preparation time: a few minutes • Cooking time: 10 minutes.

250 grams (9 oz.) dried apricots
4 tablespoons sugar
juice of 1 lemon

1. Wash the apricots, put in 2 teacups of water and soak.
2. After 4 hours, remove the seeds, add the sugar and cook for 4 minutes.
3. Pass the mixture through a sieve.
4. Cool the sauce and add the lemon juice.
5. Chill.

CHILLI OIL

Preparation time: a few minutes • Cooking time: 2 minutes • Makes 1 cup.

15 to 20 red chillies
1 cup refined oil

1. Break the red chillies into big pieces.
2. Heat the oil on a high flame and add the chillies. Immediately switch off the gas and cover.
3. After 2 hours, strain and store in a bottle.

CHILLI-GARLIC SAUCE

Preparation time: a few minutes • No cooking • Makes 1 teacup.

200 ml. (7 fl.oz.) tomato ketchup *or* fresh tomato purée
1 teaspoon chilli oil
4 teaspoons chilli sauce
½ teaspoon finely grated ginger
1 clove garlic, crushed
1 teaspoon sugar if using tomato purée
salt to taste

Mix all the ingredients and blend thoroughly.

WHITE SAUCE (FOR BAKING)

Preparation time: a few minutes ● Cooking time: 5 minutes ● Makes 2 teacups.

2 tablespoons butter
2 tablespoons plain flour
2 teacups milk
salt and pepper to taste

1. Melt the butter.
2. Add the flour and cook on a slow flame until froth appears, while stirring throughout.
3. Add the milk gradually and stir continually until the sauce thickens.
4. Add salt and pepper and mix well.

NORTH INDIAN CHAAT MASALA

Preparation time: a few minutes ● No cooking ● Makes 4 teacups.

1 teacup coriander seeds
1 teacup cumin seeds
1 teacup red chillies
1 teacup amchur powder
2 tablespoons black pepper
2 tablespoons black salt
1¾ teacups salt

1. Roast the coriander and cumin seeds.
2. Mix with the remaining ingredients and powder.

MENUS FOR SITTING DOWN MEAL

MENU 1
Watermelon and grape mint cup (*page 16*)
Creole salad (*page 23*)
Spicy pancakes (*page 54*)
East and West rice (*page 39*)
Hot fudge sundae (*page 73*)

MENU 2
French onion soup (*page 21*)
Garlic bread
Bean and vegetable salad (*page 24*)
Quick masala spaghetti (*page 41*)
Corn and spinach rice (*page 50*)
Brandy snaps with vanilla ice-cream and honey sauce (*page 77*)

COCKTAIL MENUS

MENU 1

Green goddess (*page 15*)

Citrus cooler (*page 16*)

Corn and spinach cream cracker snack (*page 108*)

Cheesy tarts (*page 106*)

Onion pancakes (*page 59*)

Mexican pizza (*page 64*)

MENU 2

Summer delight (*page 14*)

Cinderella (*page 15*)

Nachos (*page 70*)

Lettuce cups (*page 113*)

Grilled vegetable toast (*page 109*)

Corn and spinach rice balls (*page 110*)

CULINARY TERMS

appetiser	a tasty bite-size portion of food (or a small drink) served before the meal.
bake, to	to cook in an oven.
baking blind	the procedure of baking unfilled pastry cases e.g. flans, tarts etc.
batter	dry ingredients beaten or mixed with a liquid into a paste.
beat, to	a term used for introducing air into a mixture. This is done by a vigorous over and over motion of an instrument like wooden spoon, fork, wire whisk or electric beater.
blend, to	to mix ingredients until completely uniform.
boil, to	to heat to a boiling state.
brush, to	to coat thinly with a brush.
caramalise sugar, to	to heat sugar to a temperature at which a dark brown substance (caramel) is obtained.
chop, to	to cut solid food into small pieces using a very sharp knife or a processor.
churn, to	to stir vigorously.
coat, to	to cover food with a thin layer of items like butter, egg, flour, bread crumbs etc.
consistency	a term used to describe the thickness, density, texture, etc., of a mixture.
cream, to	a term used for making a mixture of fat and butter creamy (by incorporating air, breaking down the sugar crystals and softening the fat). This is done either by rubbing or by working the ingredients against the sides of the mixing bowl using a wooden spoon or fork or mixer.
croutons, bread	small cubes of crisp fried or toasted bread.
cubes	small cubical pieces of vegetables, cheese, fruit etc. usually about 12 mm. (½") on each of those sides.
deep fry, to	to cook food in a deep layer of hot fat.
dissolve, to	to stir a dry substance in a liquid until it goes into solution.
dot, to	to scatter small pieces of food like butter, nuts, chocolate etc. over the surface of a larger piece of food.

dough	a mixture of liquid and flour (and other ingredients if desired) of a sufficiently thick and pliable consistency to enable kneading and rolling out.
dredge, to	to coat food uniformly with powdered ingredients like icing sugar, flour etc.
dust, to	to sprinkle or lightly coat food with flour or sugar.
fat	a solid or semi-solid vegetable oil like butter, ghee, hydrogenated oil or margarine.
flambé, to	to prepare food by pouring a dressing of hot liquor (usually brandy) on food after lighting it and setting it aflame.
fold in, to	to combine two food items very gently with a wire whisk or spoon using an under and over motion until they are thoroughly mixed.
fry, to	to cook in a small layer of hot fat.
garnish, to	to add portions of herbs, fruit, vegetables etc. to a food dish for decoration or flavour.
grate, to	to shred food to smaller size by rubbing against an instrument with a sharp-edged surface.
grill, to	to cook directly under a flame or in an oven.
grind, to	to reduce a food to powder or paste form by crushing
herb	aromatic plant used in cookery, generally for seasoning or garnishing.
icing	a smooth covering made out of fine sugar, flavouring and colouring; also the process of applying such covering.
knead, to	to work and press a flour mixture into a uniform pliable dough mass. Use the heels of the hands whilst working in order that the dough becomes stretched and elastic.
marinate, to	to soak food in a liquid (like juice, dressing, wine etc.) with the object of transferring flavour to it.
mash, to	to beat or crush food to a soft, pulpy stage.
melt, to	to bring to liquid form by heating.
mix, to	to stir usually with a spoon with the object of combining the ingredients uniformly.
pallet knife	a flat knife without any sharp blade, used for smoothening food surfaces.
patty	a small flat cake of food. Also a small pastry shell filled with creamed food.
peel, to	to remove the outer skin or covering from a fruit, tuber etc.
pipe, to	to press material e.g. icing sugar, cream etc. through a piping bag so as to produce an ornamental pattern.
pound, to	to beat food into fine pieces or powder.
pre-heat, to	to heat an oven to a given temperature in advance (i.e. before placing the food in it for cooking).

purée	a smooth mixture obtained by reducing food like tomatoes, spinach, strawberries to a pulp.
rind	peel of a fruit, usually lemon or orange.
roast, to	to cook without fat.
roll out, to	to flatten and spread out dough into thinner layers using a cylindrical rolling pin.
rub in, to	to apply fat to a food using the fingers.
sauce	a (liquid) dressing used for imparting flavour or giving relish.
set, to	to bring a liquid to solid stae.
simmer, to	to boil gently on a slow flame.
soak, to	to keep food in a liquid until some of the latter is absorbed by it.
steam, to	to cook by means of steam, usually over a pan of boiling water in a closed vessel.
stew, to	to boil slowly in a small amount of liquid over a long period of time.
stir, to	to agitate and mix, usually with a spoon.
stock	the liquid in which food is cooked.
string, to	to remove the stringy fibres from beans etc.
unmould, to	to remove from a mould without spoiling the decorative shape.
whip, to	to make frothy and incorporate air in food like cream, egg-whites etc. by rapid agitation of whisk or similar utensil.